CHESS

2 Manuscripts:

CHESS FOR BEGINNERS

Winning Strategies and Tactics for Beginners

CHESS FOR KIDS

How to Become a Junior Chess Master

CHESS FOR BEGINNERS

Winning Strategies and
Tactics for Beginners

Table of Contents:

sources. Please consult a licensed professional before attempting any techniques outlined in this book.

By reading this document, the reader agrees that under no circumstances are is the author responsible for any losses, direct or indirect, which are incurred as a result of the use of information contained within this document, including, but not limited to, —errors, omissions, or inaccuracies.

Introduction to CHESS FOR BEGINNERS

I want to thank you for choosing this book, 'Chess mastery – winning strategies and tactics for beginners.'

Chess is an exciting game that has infinite possibilities. It is a game of strategic thinking and a game of tactics. But above all, it is a game of nerves.

The game of chess has been played all over the world for over 2000 years now. It is believed to have originated in India in the 4th century BC by a Brahman named Sissa, and was formerly called Chaturanga.

However, the first mention of the game in literary works is dated back to a Persian romance book called the Karnamak, written in around 600 AD. It was Alexander the Great who took chess to Persia when he conquered India, and from there it moved into Arabia.

Later on, chess, or Chaturanga as it was known then, traveled its way into North Africa and then Europe, at the same time spreading out to Russia as well. This meant that, before America was discovered, chess was already established and had a firm following over three continents, mainly due to a fascination with the game itself and as a way of testing mental ability.

As well as all of that, chess is a fun game. If you want to learn how to play chess, find out how all the pieces move, understand basic tactics and strategies, you have come to the right place. This book is designed to give you the basics and teach how to play chess to win.

Chapter 1: Origins of Chess

Chess is a fantastic game that helps train the brain and sharpens your mental abilities in some areas, including:

- Critical thinking
- Concentration
- Abstract reasoning
- Pattern Recognition
- Problem solving
- Creativity
- Strategic planning
- Analysis
- Evaluation
- Synthesis

And that is not all; chess is beneficial for a lot more reasons! By learning how to play chess, you can sharpen your abilities in many other areas and arenas of your day-to-day life and improve your cognitive abilities beyond your expectations.

One of the most important advantages of playing chess is that it helps enhance your problem solving ability; learning HOW to solve a problem is often far more valuable than the actual solution to the problem. Chess teaches you about how to analyze situations by placing your focus on important factors and by removing all distractions and superfluous factors from the equation. It shows you how to come up with a solution, how to think creatively and out of the box to get the perfect solution and how to put a plan into action.

Right before we delve into the details of the tactics of chess, let us have a look at how the game came into existence. The history of this game is a fascinating one. Chess has transformed over the years into the game, as we know it today. It is seldom known how this game originally started. Let us have a brief look at the transformation of chess over the centuries.

The history of chess begins nearly 1500 years ago. The earliest form of this game developed in India in as early as the 6th Century AD. It was then known as Chaturanga. Chaturanga was introduced during the time of the Guptas' rule in India. It was based on the four divisions of the army; namely the elephants, infantry, cavalry and the chariots, hence the name Chaturanga- which means "four parts."

In Chaturanga, the queen didn't exist as a piece. Instead, there was a general or counselor. There are differences between modern day chess and Chaturanga, but both can be played using the same modern day chessboard. The rules of Chaturanga vary from that of modern day chess. In Chaturanga, the soldier could move only one square as part of the initial move. However, in modern chess, we know that the pawns can move two squares, in the context of the initial move. Another major variation from modern chess is the position of the pieces on the board.

In Chaturanga, the kings are placed diagonally opposite each other on the board, unlike being placed facing each other in modern chess. In Chaturanga, the game ends when one player eliminates all the pieces of their opponent, except the king. Another difference is that in Chaturanga if a stalemate is reached, the player who is stalemated is declared the winner. These are two significant variations from the modern chess. In modern day chess, a stalemate results in a draw and not an outright win for either player.

From India, Chaturanga traveled to Persia. In Persia, Chaturanga was transformed into Shatranj. The game underwent several changes at this point. In Persia, it became popular amongst the nobility, and soon it became an integral part of the education system. Shatranj was much more similar to modern day chess than Chaturanga was. However, there still were some differences between the two versions of the game. It was at this stage in the history of the game that the concept of tactics came into play.

The position of the pieces on the board was quite similar to that of modern day chess. However, the significant difference is the one that Shatranj inherited from Chaturanga. The pawn in Shatranj was also allowed to move just one square in their initial move while modern chess allows the pawn to move two squares. Another difference that was adopted from Chaturanga was the fact that the game ended once a player eliminated all their opponent's pieces, except the king. However, the stalemate rule was the opposite of what Chaturanga rules allowed. In Shatranj, the player who stalemated their opponent wins the game instead of the stalemated opponent, which was the case in Chaturanga.

During this period, several important players emerged. It was these players who recorded the first books on tactics and strategies. From these records rose the first archives of chess literature. These books were a testimony to the growth of chess and the experience of these players. Some of the well-known players of Shatranj who emerged at this time are As-Suli Al-Razi and Rabrab.

When the Arabs conquered Persia, they took Shatranj to the entire Muslim world. By the end of 1000 AD, the game traveled to Europe and Russia, where it became very popular. From there, it spread to China and Japan. With these travels, several variations were introduced to the game; most of which aren't seen today. Between the 13th and 15th century, the game underwent several changes. The rules were changed, and more tactics were discovered. Some of these rules are still seen in today's chess game. It was during this time that modern day chess started taking shape. Most rules enforced during this period were to make sure that the game didn't take forever to complete, which is why pawns are allowed to move two squares instead of one. The concept of castling also came into existence during this time. It was also during this time that the Queen and Bishop got powers. There was a point when chess was referred to as the "Mad Queen Chess" because of the powers that were bestowed upon the queen. By the start of the 15th century, the game started looking more like the game we know today. This was when famous chess strategies and tactics came into play.

By the 19th century, modern chess tournaments were held, and the very first World Chess Championship took place in 1886. The 20th century brought with it the establishment of the World Chess Federation and by the 21st century, computers were being used for analysis of tournaments. Online gaming started in the 1990s.

The journey of chess from its primitive form as Chaturanga to the game it is today is indeed a fascinating one.

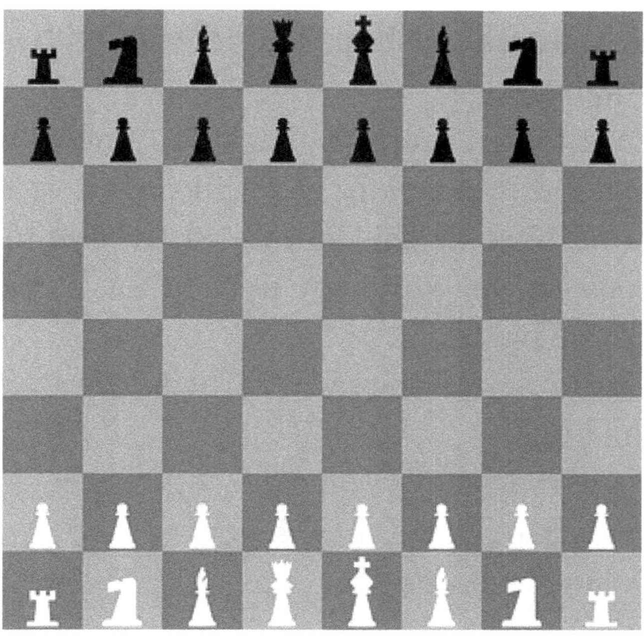

The most basic thing that you are required to learn in chess is how to set the board up. The rule here is always "white is right," and that means, when you sit in front of the board, the bottom right square should always be white. If you are playing on a board that folds in half, you must always play across the fold as well. The set up for both the black and the white pieces is the same:

- The rooks or castles must go on the two corner squares on the bottom row.
- The Knights, or horses, go on the squares directly adjacent to the rooks.
- Next are the bishops and they stand beside the knights.
- Your queen must always go on the square that matches her color. You will have two squares remaining at this point, so the white queen goes on the white square and the black queen on the black.
- The remaining square on the bottom row is for the king.

This is your first row, or rank, on the chessboard. The pawns are placed on the next row of squares in front of the bigger pieces.

How Each Chess Piece Moves

Each of the pieces has its own set of moves that it can make. No piece can move through another, but the knight can jump over other pieces. No piece can move into a square that is occupied by one of their pieces either. You can place them onto a square that is occupied by the opposition, and this is known as capturing. Your piece replaces the one you have captured, and that is removed from play. Each piece can also defend their pieces from being captured and can control vital squares or parts of the board. Let's look at the moves each separate piece can make:

The King

This is the most important piece of the board and is the point of the game – the idea being to checkmate the opponent's king in a way that they cannot get out of. However, it is also the weakest piece. Kings can move just one square in any direction – to the side, down, up or diagonally. You are not allowed to move your king into a position where it would be in check.

The Queen

This is the single most powerful piece on a chessboard. The queen can move in any direction and can move as many squares as is possible provided she does not go through any of your other pieces. As soon as she makes a capture, like all chess pieces, her move is over.

The Rook

Rooks can move as far as they want to but cannot move diagonally – only sideways, backward and forwards. These are very powerful, especially when they are used together and to protect one another.

The Bishop

The bishop is another piece that can move as far as it wants but only diagonally. Each bishop will start on a square of a particular color – one on black and one on white – and they must stay on that color throughout the game. Again, bishops work well together because they can cover one another.

The Pawn

The pawn is one of the most unusual pieces on the board because of the way it moves and captures pieces. Many people see the pawn as an inconsequential piece but, when used correctly, it can be one of the strongest pieces you have in your army. Pawns can only move one square at a time except for their very first move when they can go two squares. To capture another piece, the pawn has to do so diagonally, never forwards, backward or sideways. If the pawn is blocked by another piece in front, it cannot move past it nor can it take it.

Chapter 3: Comprehension of Basic Chess Rules

The game of chess is won when you force your opponent's king into checkmate, which means they have to be captured. A checkmate is a position in which the owner of the king cannot make any move whatsoever to get their king to safety, be it moving the king or moving another piece in to defend it. If a player makes a move against their opponent's king and leaves in such a way that the king can be captured on the next move, this is called check, and the opponent must save their king on their next move.

The king is never actually physically captured. It is the responsibility of both players to ensure that there are no available moves that will help stop the king being captured or put into checkmate. When you place your opponent's king into check, you must say the word "check." This will warn the other player that their king is in danger. Likewise, if you place their king into checkmate, you must say, "checkmate" when you do it. One thing you must never do is expose your king in such a way that your opponent can place it into check.

As you play the game, you must try to capture your opponent's pieces to get them out of the game. This clears the way for you to attack their king with the least amount of opposition. To capture a piece, you move onto the square that the piece occupies and replace it with your piece. You cannot capture your own, and you cannot have two of your pieces on the same square,

White always starts the game of chess and, from then on, each player takes in turns to move a piece. You must make a move on every turn. There is no such thing as passing in a chess game unless you are castling. This is a particular move made in which two pieces are moved in a bid to protect the king – this move will be explained in greater detail a little later.

Be aware that not every game will end in a win for someone. Some games end up as draws or ties. These are called stalemates, and it occurs when neither player has their king in check, but neither can make a legal move without placing their king into check. Remember, you cannot put yourself in check and, if your only move would let that happen, the game must end in a stalemate.

Special Moves

There are a couple of special moves and abilities that some pieces have in a game of chess, and you would do well to learn them and use them.

Promotion

This only applies to pawns. No other piece has this unique ability. If you can get one of your pawns successfully across the chessboard to the other side, it can be promoted into any other piece you desire. This means that you can promote it into any piece on the board. Most people choose to promote their pawns to queens as it gives them a distinct advantage. It is also not true that you can promote your pawn only to a piece that has already been captured by your opponent. If you are talented enough and plan your game carefully, you can end up having multiple queens on the board.

En Passant

This also applies only to pawns. En Passant means "in passing" in French and, in this move, if you move your pawn two squares out on its first move and that move puts you directly beside your opponent's pawn, the opponent can use his pawn to capture yours. As a rule, pawns can only capture diagonally unless this situation arises. In a typical situation, your opponent can capture your pawn only if it is diagonal to his pawn. Using this method, your opponent can capture your pawn when you are next to his pawn. However, that pawn must be captured on the next move. Otherwise, it cannot be done. A player doesn't necessarily have to capture his opponent's pawn if he has a better move, but if this is the only legal move, then he must capture his opponent's pawn. This is the only capture move where the piece that captures does not take the place of the captured piece.

Castling

This is the move that allows you to move two pieces in one go. First and foremost, it is a move designed to keep your king safe or to move it to safety if need be. Secondly, it also allows you to bring the rook away from the corner square and into play. When it is your turn, and you chose to castle, you move your king two squares to the side - either side- and then move the rook to the other side of the king. For example, move your king from E1 to G1 and then move the rook from H1 to F1. Some conditions must be true to the castle:

- This must be the very first move that your king makes
- It must also be the very first move that the rook makes
- Castling can't be done if there are any pieces between the king and the rook
- The king cannot be in check or cannot pass through check

When you castle to the side that the king is nearest to, this is called castling kingside. When you castle to the side that the queen is on, this is called Castling queenside. Irrespective of which side you choose to go, you may still only move the king two squares.

Check and Checkmate

As I explained earlier, the purpose of a game of chess is to place your opponent's king into checkmate, a position whereby the king cannot be moved to safety and another piece cannot be brought in to play to defend it. There are just three ways in which an opponent can get their king out of check:

- Move to another position without castling
- Use another piece to block the checkmate
- Capture the piece that is threatening the checkmate

Draws

Sometimes a chess game will go to a tie or a draw. It is essential for you to know about these draws if you want to avoid them. If you remain unaware of them, your opponent could push a game that you could have won easily one into a draw. Here are five reasons why that may happen:

- A stalemate is reached where neither person can move without putting their king into check (the king will NOT be in check at this point)

I am sure that you are aware of what a stalemate entails. While under a stalemate, the opponent's king isn't threatened in any way. However, your opponent has no legal moves left. Beginners usually opt for this method to end the game in a draw. Professionals know that the chances of players making silly mistakes to end up in a stalemate are very slim. Hence, they stay away from it. However, there have been instances where professional players end games in a stalemate.

- The two players can agree to draw and halt the game

This is one of the easiest ways to draw a game. According to this method, both players mutually agree to a draw. This happens only when both players feel that they have no chance of winning. Such a situation arises when a player feels that he can win only if his opponent messes it up. When you play on a professional platform, you know that the chances of your opponent making a silly mistake are highly unlikely. This is when you offer an option to draw the game. This way both of you end up with one point each. There are many instances where the players call it a draw because of the cash prize involved. Some tournaments offer both players' cash prize if the game ends in a draw. This is why a lot of tournaments end with a draw because it benefits both players. However, the players are not allowed to call a draw even before the game begins.

- There are insufficient pieces left on the chessboard to force a checkmate.

This situation arises when both players are left with very few pieces. When both players have very few pieces, it becomes impossible for them to checkmate their opponent's king. Hence, due to the lack of pieces, the players can end in a draw. Some guidelines need to be met before a player can claim a draw through this method. This rule can be used only if it is not at all possible for the player to checkmate his opponent's king, even after some legal moves. It is tough for players to prove that they don't have enough pieces to checkmate their opponent. Hence this method of the draw isn't used very often.

- If the same position is declared three times, not necessarily in a row, a player may declare a draw.

This is a situation known as threefold repetition. When a player makes the same move thrice in a match, the opponent can claim a draw. The procedure to claim this draw is different from the others. However, the principle behind all the draws is the same. This rule cannot be used to claim a draw after three checks because a player usually checks his opponent some times throughout a match. However, if a player gives you a check in the same manner thrice in a row, then you can use this rule to declare a draw.

- 50 moves have been played consecutively without either player capturing a piece or moving a pawn.

Not many players know this rule, or even if they do, they do not understand how it works. According to this rule, if in a specific game, the game shows no sign of progress for both players at the end of fifty moves each, then either one of the players can claim to end the game in a draw. When I say progress, it means the movement of a pawn or the loss of a piece. If the game doesn't show any such signs of progress, then the game can end in a draw. However, this rarely happens because no professional player would make fifty useless moves. In a game between two beginners, such a situation could arise.

Tips to draw a game:

Now that you have seen the various situations under which a draw might be offered let's have a look at some tips that can help you out in these situations. Such tips will allow you to claim a draw without antagonizing or hurting your opponent's sentiments. It is up to you to reject or accept the claim of a draw. However, you could do it with some grace so that you don't offend your opponent. These tips will help you draw a game with ease and tact.

- Only on your move.

You should make a claim to a draw only during your turn. There are two main reasons why you should make this offer only during your turn. They are:

i. It is considered rude if you offer a draw during your opponent's turn. This is because your opponent will be distracted by your offer and may end up losing precious time. It will look as if you were trying to intentionally distract him. He will not only get offended, he might even raise objections. Since tournaments are clocked, he will lose out on precious seconds by trying to interpret your claim. If he is distracted, it will definitely be an advantage to you. Hence, to avoid misunderstandings, you should claim only during your turn.

ii. When you make the claim during your opponent's turn, he will doubt your claim and start analyzing the reasoning behind it. He will look at your weak points and as to why you claimed the draw. Hence, it could possibly lead to him making an aggressive move, which could make the game worse for you.

- Plan your move first

Not many players understand how these claims for a draw are made and forget about the clock. Hence, they forget to stop the clock and lose precious time. This is why most beginners lose time even before their opponent has a chance to accept or reject the claim for a draw. The ideal way to claim a draw is to make your move, then make the offer to draw and immediately click the clock so that the opponent has to think over the offer during his turn and not during yours. This way, you don't waste time and your opponent doesn't take advantage of your offer by not letting you play while he considers the offer. If your opponent continues playing without replying to your offer, it is a clear sign that he has rejected your offer to draw.

- Never draw a strong opponent

It is rude to claim a draw when your opponent is a strong player. Your opponent might actually get offended. You may wonder how to figure if your opponent is strong or not. A glance at his ratings should tell you if he is a strong player or not. If your opponent's ratings are higher than yours by at least more than four hundred or five hundred points, then it is safe to say that he is a strong player. While the main reason to avoid presenting a draw to a strong player is that it is offensive, there are various other reasons as well. These other reasons are:

i. If your player is strong, he will realize that a draw will benefit you the most and that he would most likely beat you if the game continued. He will look for your weaknesses and try to attack you at your weak points. He will not consider accepting your offer of a draw.

ii. You can learn a lot from your opponent, especially if you are a beginner or if he is a stronger player than you. If you offer a draw to end the game, you lose out on information and tips that you could have learnt from your opponent if you had continued the game. Your growth as a player is also important and the only way you will grow is, if you play as many games as possible and observe your opponents during those games. If you can't observe your opponents, you will not grow.

- Don't offer draws repeatedly during a game

Never offer draws repeatedly during a game. Make an offer once during a game. If your opponent rejects it, then stop making offers again and just try to come up with strategies to beat him. Do not make another offer unless something changes in the fundamentals of the game and you find a situation where you feel the opponent might be more likely to accept your offer. When you make repeated offers, your opponent tends to feel threatened. This will only distract them and make them lose time. Since time matters a lot in chess, your offers might make your opponent lose. When you do it repeatedly and your opponent looks visibly harassed, then the tournament authorities may consider it as an offense and might even bar you from the game. Hence, make sure that you do not offer draws repeatedly in a game.

- Reject offers politely

When your opponent offers you a draw and you feel like you could win and want to reject the draw, make sure you do so politely. Don't make an unnecessary fuss about his offer. He might have offered the draw just to benefit from it rather than distract you. Hence, make sure you react politely to your opponent's offer to draw. If your opponent constantly harasses you with offers, then you can get in touch with the tournament director or organizers to resolve the problem rather than responding in a rude manner.

These tips will certainly be useful to you when you have to deal with draws in a tournament. They will help you deal with draws in a diplomatic and amicable manner. Therefore, make sure you follow them whether you offer a draw or if you are being offered a draw. These small reactions go a long way in how people perceive you and will give others the idea that you don't let emotions cloud your judgment.

Understanding Chess Notation

There are a various types of notations in chess, depending on the language spoken and whether you are playing against a real person or a computer. The most universally used notation is algebraic, as everyone understands this. The algebraic notation uses one letter and one number for each square and a letter for the chess piece.

The board numbering and lettering is biased towards the white side as this is always the starting side and goes as such:

- Starting on the bottom left corner and working horizontally across the board are the letters "a" through to "h" – these are known as "files"
- Starting in the same square and working vertically up the board are the numbers "1" through to "8" – these are known as "ranks"
- Thus, the bottom left hand square as you face the board from the white side is "a1".

Each chess piece is also given a letter:

- King – (K)
- Queen – (Q)
- Bishop – (B)
- Knight – (N) – because K is already in use by the King
- Rook – (R)
- Pawn – none

The letters that represent pieces are always capitalized and the square letters are in lower case.

If a piece captures another piece, the notation includes an "x" in front of the square the capture was made on, i.e. Bxe5 denotes that a Bishop captured a piece on square e5. If a pawn is responsible for a capture, the notation includes the file from which the pawn started on, i.e. exd5 denotes that a pawn on file e captured a piece on d5.

Chapter 4: Opening Moves in Chess

Theoretically, you can start the chess game with any move as far as it is a legal move according to the rules regarding the movements of the pieces. The first move, which is known as the opening move, should be a good move as it gives an edge over the opponent as you have an upper hand with the good opening move. A better opening move actually gives you an opportunity to protect the king, to make utmost use of the vital squares, to move the pieces in the desired direction, to swap and capture the pieces as per the rules.

After studying the game of chess for many decades, moves are provided with a name, in order to identify the moves without much difficulty. As I will be explaining the famous opening moves that have been repeatedly used over the years, I would recommend laying the chess board and placing the pieces as it will be easy to make the moves and understand the situation as explained.

To start with the opening moves, here is a brief of three popular sets of openings:

1. The white will begin with moving the Pawn of the King to E4. This move facilitates an opportunity to make use of the Bishop and the Queen for the next move and also opens up the center of the board. It is considered as a popular move as gives two option to the black

   i. ¤ The first option is to move as same as the white by taking King's Pawn to e5. By this move, black also acquires the advantage enjoyed by the white as it gives an opportunity to the black to operate the center. Ruy Lopez, King's Gambit and Giuoco Piano have such opening.

  ii. ¤ The second option is to make an unique opening move in the form of Silican Defense, Caro-Kann, French Defense, Pirc or Modern and Center Counter instead of the popular moves.

2. Openings of King's Indian Defense, Queen's gambit, Nimzo-Indian and Queen's Indian Defense can be followed by the white through moving the Queen's Pawn to d4.

3. The English Opening can be followed without making a move to E4 or d4.

Ruy Lopez

Spanish Opening is the other name of Ruy Lopez. The three initial moves in this opening are:

1. E4 e5
2. Nf3 Nc6
3. Bb5

The name of the opening is derived from a Spanish clergyman who lived in the 16th Century, as he was a true enthusiast of the game. It is considered as one of the pioneer moves in the early days of chess. Lopez used to record the moves in his notebook after closely studying the openings of chess. He has used over 150 pages for the documentation of openings in the history of chess. Even though this move has his name, it is considered to be an older move that was developed even before he was born. The proof to the statement is that, this opening move has been mentioned in a Gottingen manuscript of 1490.

Only because of Jaenisch, a Russian Theoretician in mid of 1800, this move came into existence again until then Lopez opening was infamous. Many Grandmasters make use of this opening, as it is a preferred move of the present generation players.

A potential pin is enforced by the white by making use of the d-pawn or Knight and castle is activated as the open attack is launched. The black is forced to move its e-pawn to d4 by the opening of the white.

Giuco Piano

This type of opening move is also known as 'Quiet game'. The Bishop of the white is used for the attack. The counter-attack by the black is done easily by making use of moves such as

1. E4 e5
2. Nf3 Nc6
3. Bc4 Bc5

The game becomes passive when the white tackles by moving to d3. Such a move is known as 'Giuoco Pianissimo' or 'The Quietest Game'. But, the move can be Evans Gambit when the white moves to b4 instead of d3. This move facilitates exchange of pawn in order to get access to center of the board and the Queen's Bishop is unlocked and ready for action.

King's Gambit

This was a favorite move of 1800's players as it was the most used opening move of those times. The white gets to exchange a pawn in order to gain control over the game immediately by taking a lead. The black can tackle the move easily without any loss. Hence, King's Gambit is no longer much utilized in the professional level games of today. The moves to open with are:

1. E4 e5
2. F4

The next move will be exf4 for the Gambit.

Sicilian Defense

Widely used move of the Grandmasters and the opening move will be:

1. E4 c5

The black as a reply will try to take control of the center by bringing into play the c-file in place of repeating the moves of the white. Such a move will complicate the play as the pattern of the pieces may take any direction. The black will capture the e4 pawn of the white by taking the Knight to f6 and Bishop to b7. Black will love a move to d5 without a risk.

There are various other options in Sicilian Defense, if analyzed closely with regard to the moves. The widely used move being 'the dragon' which begins with

1. E4 c5

2. Nf3 d6
3. D4 cxd4
4. Nxcd4 NF6
5. Nc3 g6

The reason for the name is the formation of the black pawns, after the moves, resembles the shape of the dragon.

'Najdorf' is also a famous option that is similar to the dragon. The only difference in between the options is the last step.

1. E4 c5
2. Nf3 d6
3. D4 cxd4
4. Nxcd4 NF6
5. Nc3 a6

French Defense

Black gives a window for the white to operate in the center as in the time being, black will have wall around its pieces with the help of the pawns to safeguard. The opening moves will be

1. E4 e6
2. D4 d5

As the game proceeds, the pawns of the either party will be competing to have a control over the game as the lead swings here and there. Both players look to outplay the other in order to gain a greater position in the game. The move to e5 is expected from the white and a move to c5 or f6 is expected from the black. The Queen Bishop of the black is known to the 'French Bishop' as it is commonly trapped in this type of opening.

Caro-Kann

The black gives space to white to capture the center as the black makes a move to the d5 by employing the pawn. This opening is just like the French Defense with an extra move. The moves to start with are

1. E4 e6
2. D4 d5
3. Nc3 dxe4

The pawns of the white are attacked by the black in order to bring in play his pieces to take control of the board. Such a move is not a part of French defense if comparing both the openings. Black will end up playing a passive game with hope of white making a minor mistake in order to get into the game again.

Center Counter

The 'Scandinavian Opening' is the other name of Center Counter that opens with:

1. E4 e5

And the next move will mostly be exd5 Qxd5

Pric or Modern

Commonly known by the names such as Pric or Modern and is started with either of the following two moves:

1. E4 d6

OR

1. E4 g6

The variation of the Modern Defense can begin with:

1. E4 g6

2. D4 Bg7

In 1930s, this move was considered as an ineffective move. But, since 1960s, the risk-taking players have played this move. The white is given a chance to make use of the center by the black with an intention of outsmarting the white in the process.

Such a tricky move needs a lot of courage, as center is not in the control of the player.

Queen's Gambit

Done with the opening move of e4, now comes the other moves. The opening moves of Queen's Gambit are:

1. D4 d5
2. C4

The exchange of pawn will be the option for the white. Whereas, the black is left with various options such as:

1. Dxc4- the risky move where the Queen's Gambit is accepted
2. Nc6 - known as the 'Tchigoran Defense'
3. E6 - ending up in 'Tarrasch Defense'
4. E6 - 'Orthodox Defense'

King's Indian Defense

In the opening of this method, the black plays the role of underdog by letting the white to dominate the center with the view of exploiting the advantage gained by the white to win the game. Many Grandmasters employ such an opening in spite of being risky. The opening moves include:

1. D4 Nf6
2. c4 g6
3. Nc3 Bg7

Later, the reply of black will be c5 and white will move to d5. Following which black will take back the piece to e6 and then to b5.

Queen's Indian Defense, Bogo-Indian and Nimzo-Indian

These are the three types of Indian openings of defense that have a similar starting move, such as:

1. D4 Nf6
2. c4 e6

Nc3 Bb4 is followed by Nimzo - Indian, as the pawns of the white will try to control center with the powerful pieces just behind the pawns.

Dutch defense

The initial move will be

1. D4 f5

The attack is launched by the black with the aim of proceeding towards the white's king along with defeating the army pieces of the white in the initial stage of the game. Conversely, at the same time, the vulnerability of the black is exposed when the attack is on from the beginning. The f-pawn of the black will be a hindrance for the other pieces to take control of the center.

English opening

'Flank maneuver' is the other name of English opening, which has a unique opening such as:

1. c4

The attempt to take control of center is made by white through taking charge of the sides. Whereas, c5 is the option left for the black as a counter.

The King's Indian Attack

In order to give a sound reply to King's Indian Defense, this attack is played to gain an edge over the opponent. The sequence of play is:

- E4, d3
- Nd2, Ngf3
- G3, Bg2
- 0-0

The white has an upper hand with these moves. The black will look to employ the French Defense or Sicilian Defense in order to tackle the strong opening move of the white. Nevertheless, black cannot surpass the white, as the opening move is stronger to tackle the counters of the black. The center may witness a harsh play, as many pieces could be lost in the attack for both the players.

The distinct feature of this opening is that, it has a capacity of being played even in the middle of the game and not just in the beginning of the game. The black should have a sound proof strategy in order to fight back against the white who can use this counter to a defensive of the black. This counter will actually help the white to proceed an all-out to the king of the black.

Alekhine's Defense

This move came into play in the year 1921, is considered as a hypermodern move of defense which includes moves such as:

E4

Nf6

The move opens the door of being aggressive for the black. Such a forceful move makes white form a broad pawn formation to tackle to attack of the black. Black makes uses of the opportunity to gain a lead by attacking the white pieces. The opening of the white can be neutralized by such an effective black attack. Equal chances of winning are available for both players with this move.

Before bringing into play any of the pieces, make sure you think out the response and counter to the response of the move. The above-mentioned moves are the various openings and counters used over the course of the long history of chess, and you should be well versed with them in order to master the game of chess.

Chapter 5: Strategies in Chess

The words 'Chess Strategy' are very commonly used by the Chess Enthusiasts. It is basically a plan laid by the players, which addresses matters such as how to play, what moves to be made using the various pieces and at what time the moves should be made. Only a foolproof Chess Strategy can give desired result in the actual game. We will be discussing all the elements that will help to implement a successful strategy. Every move can be planned to control the game, right from the first move. But, success does not rely on just strategy, as even tackling the opponent's strategy is vital.

The knowledge about the pieces will not make you a Grandmaster, as it is important to make use of the pieces in the right way at the right time to your advantage. The opening move plans and strategy principles are explained below for you to get a better knowledge about the game before playing it.

As a beginner, it is considered important to know the guidelines until you become an expert. These are not a compulsory set of rules to be followed by all.

The Value of Chess Pieces

Every single piece in the Chessboard has a value. It differs from one unit to another depending on the command it has on the game. That said, the game of Chess is not value-oriented, as the leading points do not choose the winner. But, knowing about the value will portray the importance of each piece in Chessboard.

The Pawn is valued at 1 point each. The Knight is considered to be worth of 3 points each. The same goes for the Bishop, as it is valued at 3 points. The Rook has a massive 5 points. Lastly, the Queen has 9 points, which is more than a Rook, and a Bishop put together. The King does not need to be valued as it cannot be captured nor a value is essential, as we all know the game revolves around it.

The estimation of each piece can be understood with the above details about the pieces. This information should be considered before making a move or trading a piece in the process of the game. The status each piece enjoys in the game cannot be better explained. So, a Rook, which is estimated as 5 points, should not be sacrificed in the cause of a pawn, which is just worth of a point. But, in the same place, letting go of a Rook in the cause of capturing two Bishops of the enemy is considered a profitable trade as the opponent loses 6 points whereas we lose just 5 points. Another important reason for the trade is that the opponent will be losing two pieces of same kind.

Other reasons to affect the value of each piece:

- The single linked pawn is considered worthy than doubled pawns
- The two Bishops together have more value than a two Knight or a Bishop and a Knight together.
- The Three minor pieces is the pair of Bishops and Knights moving together is considered as a dangerous combo than a Rook pain or the Queen alone for the attack on the opposition.

The ten tips to win a Chess game

The game of Chess can be classified into three distinct stages. The first stage is known as the opening, where calculated opening moves are made to have an upper hand over the opposition. The second stage is known as middle stage, where the players play for control and position in the board by attack, counter and defense. The last stage is the endgame where the Kings come into play where saving the King becomes the motive along with the strategy to Checkmate the opponent.

In the process of the game, pieces will be captured by both the parties. Each player loves to capture more pieces than his rival to dominate the game. As we get to indulge in over thinking, we may place our own piece in danger of capture by mistake. Such an inviting capture is known as 'En Prise' or 'In Take'. But, in some cases, players voluntarily place their pieces for intake as a part of their strategy with a view to trap the opponent when he captures the piece.

Following are the top ten tips that will lead you to a victory in a game of chess:

1. Be more cautious of the moves taken by opposition than your own moves

Make sure you always take time to think about the following questions once your opponent makes a move

- What is the reason behind moving that piece?
- Is there any risk to my piece or any piece of the opposition?
- Should I be cautious of any other danger which I did not see coming?

- What can be the Strategy of my opposition?

After answering all the questions, make your move that will be a reply to the questions by spoiling the plan of the opponent.

2. Make sure to reply with the best move each time

While contemplating your own move ask yourself the following question:

- Can this piece be moved from this place to a better place?
- Can an improved effectiveness of a piece lead to a better position?
- Is this move capable of tackling the tactics of the opponent?
- Is the new position safe for this piece?
- Is the new position safe from attack if a pawn is moved?
- Is the piece worthy of the move and will it be chased by the opposition?

Emanuel Lasker, a former Chess champion, has an advice for all the Chess enthusiasts out there. He said "When you see a good move, wait- look for a better one!" In spite of it being a great move, it may not be the right time to make that move.

3. Play with a plan

As a chess player, it is very important to make moves according to the action plan. Moving around the chessboard without any precise plan will only lead to defeat as the opponent will not face challenge from your side. Each piece should be moved according to a plan and played together as a team. Just like an Orchestra that plays the same tune, chess pieces should play for the same plan.

Plan causes unity of the chess pieces. It is more impactful to attack the King of the opposition together as an army than attacking as a single piece that would be captured in a losing cause. The strategy can be to capture a certain area of the board in order to dominate the game. The plan can differ from a person to person, but it should be a well thought out plan.

4. Knowledge of each piece

The value of the pieces should be considered over the fact of number of pieces each player has in the game before trading a piece. The player who has more total value of the pieces over the other has an upper hand.

The pawn is considered as the least effective piece as it has just a point value and also, it cannot be moved backward, unlike other pieces which can be moved in the desired direction according to the movements of the pieces. Hence, this estimation of total value to know the position of the players is a good assessment. The value of three pawns will equal the worth of one Bishop or Knight. The Knight has the unique power to jump over other pieces. The Bishops move along the diagonal squares. The Bishop in the black square can move only on the black square and likewise for the Bishop in the white square. But, Bishop can move faster than the Knight.

The Rook has the power of moving around the length of the board in a short time. The value of a single Rook is equal to five pawns. The opponent's Rook can be captured using a combination of Bishop and Knight.

The worth of a Queen is equal to nine pawns, which is equal to the value of a pair of Rooks. The Queen can move in any direction across the squares of the board.

The King is the piece around which the game is played. But, it has no value or worth since it cannot be captured or traded in process of the game.

5. Well-development of the pieces.
The time factor is considered to be vital element to take control of game. The faster the pieces are developed, better is the chance for the player to dominate the proceedings of the game. Control of the board is only possible with quickly well-developed pieces brought into the play.

As a beginner, the players may waste time by moving the pawns and capturing the spaces in the board. But, the game cannot be controlled by just making the pawn movements. Make use of other pieces, which can attack more valuable pieces of the opponent, even when they are at a distance, due to the reach they have. The stronger pieces should be brought into action as soon as possible by removing the pawns that are in the way. Also, make sure that the valuable pieces do not face any danger in the process, as the opponent will keenly watch all your moves to quickly eliminate the stronger pieces. The pawns can be moved according to the plan after the valuable pieces come out for the play.

It is a common temptation to the players to bring the Queen into the play. The Queen is the key piece, which can win you the game. It is essential to make use of it only when it is the right time and place. If the Queen is lost in the initial stage of the game, it will be great loss for the player and greatest trade to the opponent. Make the moves when it is the best for the piece to attain the desired place to attack in few moves. The calculated moves will save the time of the player and the opposition.

6. Control the center

The four square of the center should be controlled in order to dominate the game. Firstly, when a piece is in the center, it can actually make more movements than in any other position of the board. For example, a Knight in the center can more in eight distinct positions as compared to a Knight in a corner, which can move to only two positions on the whole board.

Being in center also facilitates the advantage of faster movement. A piece can be taken to the opponent's territory easily when the center is in your control. The player who first captures the center can launch the attack first as the travel of the pieces is easier.

7. Safeguard the King

The ultimate aim in the game of Chess is to Checkmate the King of the opposition. Sometimes we get so occupied with the plans of defeating your opponent that we forget that our opposition is also playing with same aim.

Always ensure the safety of the King by castling it on the board. The pawns around the King are the lifesavers. Movement of such pawns should be minimal as the King will be in danger once pawns are moved away. Apply the same strategy to attack your opponent by forcing the movement of the pawns surrounding the King.

8. Timing of trading the pieces

Full use of a trading opportunity should be made when a piece of lower value can be traded in exchange of a higher value piece of the opponent. But, such chances do not arise if you are playing against a skillful opposition. So, in most cases, only an exchange of equal value is possible and the decision should be made on whether the capture is worth the lost or not.

Without a clear-cut benefit, do not risk the exchange of pieces when you have an edge over the opponent.

The attack is weakened by the factor of having lesser pieces in play and the defenders face the threat.

Trading should not be carried on when there is not much place to move your pieces in opponent's area. Only when the spaces open up, it is beneficial for the player to attack.

The pawn formation of the opponent can be affected by the trading done by the player. A situation where you can get a piece when your opponent is eligible for only a double pawn is advantageous in your cause.

9. Work on the endgame

Concentration on the endgame should always be in mind of the player from the very first move. Every move should be played with the determination to acquire the desired endgame result. For instance, a Knight and Bishop are considered to be similar in the initial stage. But, at the time of endgame, Knight would move slowly as compared to the Bishop, which strikes with a single move. So, if a decision has to be made on trading of a Bishop in place of a Knight then think about the effect of the pieces during the endgame.

Pawn structure is also a critical element when it comes to the endgame. Usage of a pawn to capture a piece of the opposition will lead to exposure of file which in turn opens up the way for movement of the Queen and Rooks. It may result in double pawn that cannot be defended by either party. The endgame has to be well fought in this case.

Both, the short term and long term goal should be taken into consideration while making a move in order to emerge as a winner.

10. Concentration

A lapse of concentration is what the opposition is looking to exploit in order to dominate the game. A move that would cause trouble will be played making use of the lapse in concentration. It is essential to be alert all time to have the game in control. If you are distracted, you may also make a move that you will end up regretting later in the game.

11. Avoid unnecessary risk

Aggression is seen as winning quality as far as it is supported by a strong plan. But, if the aggressive move is made without a plan, you will land yourself in trouble. Unnecessary risks, rather than helping you win the game, may lead you to a sorry loss. Calculated risks will help you, while reckless moves will only help the opponent to dominate the game.

12. Avoid unnecessary checks

The Checks given to the opponent's King should put the opponent in danger. The Checks should be backed with a valid plan that will help to control the game. The unnecessary Checks will be a waste of time for the player as well as the opposition when the Check does not threaten. But, in that time you can actual try a productive move that will lead to a checkmate.

13. Seizing the open files

Always make sure of occupying the open file when an opportunity arises. The player who seizes open files is always in an advantageous position over the opponent. Such a file that is seized will help in the endgame during the checkmate.

Principles and Strategies of Chess

Following are the essential principles of chess:

- Do not make the mistake of moving the same piece twice in the beginning of the game

- Make sure to develop the Bishops after developing the Knights
- Queen Bishop should be developed after the development of both the Knights
- The development should be made across the board and not just in an area
- In the opening, do not take any of your pieces to the other side
- Make sure that your King is not filed once you are done with the castling
- Wait for the castling of the opponent before pinning the Knight
- Avoid trades that will help the development of opposition's pieces
- Avoid early attack on the opponent

In this chapter, we will be discussing the following basic chess tactics and how they can be used to make your game better:

- Battery Attack
- Discovered Attack
- Discovered Check
- Fork Attack
- Pin Attack
- Skewer Attack

There are many more tactics in chess, but to understand and learn the more complex chess tactics you will need to know these basic tactics and these tactics will be taught to you with the help of simple and comprehensible animated diagrams. Now let us take a look at the aforementioned basic chess tactics.

Battery Attack

Battery attack is of a two kind attack, which comprises of Queen along with Bishop or Rook. In the first kind of attack, the Queen and the Bishop are placed side by side on the Diagonals. In the second kind, the queen is with the rook on the Straights or Ranks or Files.

As the strength of a household battery is increased when an extra cell is added, likewise, this tactics aims in strengthening the army attack with extra pieces.

Queen and Bishop's Battery

The Diagonals are made use of for this kind of battery. The Bishop is employed as it has greater reach. But, whatever is the tactic, only the board positioning will allow the player to take the calculated risk required for this kind of attack. The position of the board is explained with the diagram below for better understanding.

Queen and Rook's Battery

The Rank or File is made use of for this kind of battery attack where Queen and Rook are employed to add power. It is recommended to make the desired moves with the Rook rather than the Queen, in spite of it being the chief of the battery attack.

Chess Tactics

Queen and 2x Rooks - Battery

A battery attack with a Queen along with 2 Rooks is considered as the powerful commanding attack, which will give you an advantage over your opponent.

Alexander Alekhine applied such an attack where the Queen and two Rooks on the file move towards the rival when he plays the game of Chess. Hence, Alekhine's gun became another name of this attack.

Chess Tactics

2x **Rooks- Battery**

Without a Queen, only 2 Rooks on the Ranks or Files can form a battery attack, which can control the board. It is very effective in spite of being a weaker battery attack as compared to the aforementioned 3 kinds of attack. But, only the game situation can determine the level of effectiveness of such an attack.

Chess Tactics

Discovered Attack

The two different units of the two opposing players are against each other but the King of the either players are not attacked.

One unit comes into play when the other unit is pulled out of the way. Only then the unit can attack the opponent, such is the case of discovered unit.

From the image below, we can understand that Bishop is the uncovered unit or can be called as discovered unit in this scenario.

Chess Tactics

Discovered Check

Unlike Discovered Attack, in Discovered Check the King is in danger. The discovered unit attacks the enemy King in this case.

Since, the black should save the King according to the diagram. The discovered unit has actually enforced a Check that leads to sacrifice of Black Queen in an attempt to save the King. At the same time when the white Bishop checks the King, the Queen is under the radar of the white Knight.

Chess Tactics

Fork attack

In this case, a single unit has the capacity to attack two rival units in one move.

Two Chess Tactics such as Relative Fork and Absolute Fork are explained below with images

Chess Tactics

Relative Fork Attack

The Relative Fork Attack is basically an attack made by one unit on two or more pieces of the opponent in a single tactic that excludes the rival King. It is up to the opponent to decide which piece he wants to rescue and which piece will face the attack. The following diagram shows how a single move of white's Queen can put the Rook and the Knight of the Black in danger.

Absolute Fork Attack

In the case of Absolute Fork Attack, the King of the enemy is attacked along with another piece or pawn of the opponent in a single move. Since, opponent should save King as the King is checked and leave other piece in danger.

The image shows that the white Queen can attack the black King and the Rook at the same time.

Chess Tactics

Pin attack

This attack comes into play when a lesser important piece or pawn is ahead of an important piece.

There are two types of Pin Attack in form of Relative and Absolute Pin Attack.

Relative Pin Attack

The less important pawn or piece is attacked if it is before an important key piece. And since, it is a relative attack the important piece is not the King of the rival player.

The white Knight in this case is the pinned unit. The movement of such a unit may disturb the formation to safeguard more valuable pieces and put such pieces in danger.

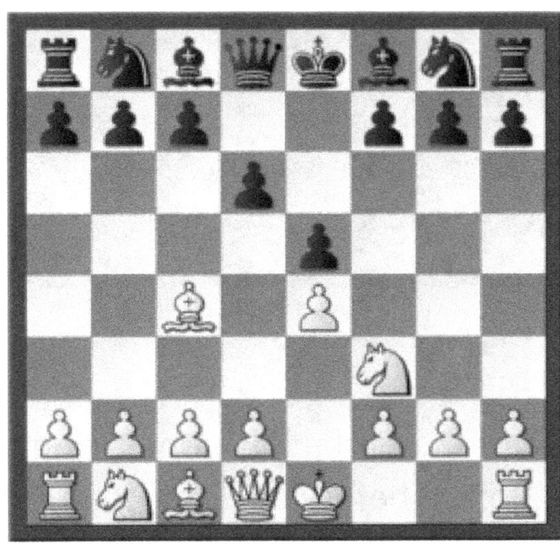

Chess Tactics

Absolute Pin Attack

As the attack is absolute, the King is in danger. The pinned unit cannot move, as the protection of the King is prime cause of the game. If such a piece tries to move, it is illegal against the rules of the Chess where voluntary Check is impossible.

In this scenario, the black Queen should be pinned to the black King due to the white Rook.

Chess Tactics

Skewer Attack

The identification of attack is done through presence of important piece before a lesser important piece or pawn.

The Relative and Absolute Skewer Attacks are discussed briefly below.

Relative Skewer Attack

The attack is launched on a valuable unit with the view of capturing the lesser valuable unit just behind the valuable unit. This attack facilitates the movement of important piece that was a hindrance to attack the lesser valuable piece or pawn.

The white Bishop looking to capture the black Knight should first threaten the black Rook.

Chess Tactics

Absolute Skewer Attack

The enemy King is attacked with a Check in order to capture lesser valuable piece behind the King. When a Check is enforced, the opponent should save the King by moving if impossible to block with a piece. In that situation, the movement of King opens up the chance to attack the pieces just behind the King.

According to the image, the Rook should be exposed to danger in an attempt to save the King from Check. The white Queen would easily capture the Rook once the King is off the way.

Chess Tactics

Chapter 7: Glossary

Here are certain terms or words that you will come across constantly in Chess and it is better that you get acquainted with them before you start playing chess so that you have an edge over your opponent.

- Active Piece – A chess piece that has complete and free range of the chess board
- Attack – The act of going after opposing pieces, specifically the King
- Battery – Two of the long ranging pieces lined up in the same direction on a diagonal, rank or file, like a Queen and a Bishop
- Blockade - When you put a piece into the path of a "passed pawn" so that it cannot go for promotion
- Blunder – A bad move that can cost you either the game or some serious pieces
- Castling – A move that involves your King and one of your Rooks and is made to put your King in a safe position. The only move in the game in which a player can make two moves

- Center - d4, e4, d5 and e5 – the four-center square of the board
- Check - An attack or threat that is made directly on the King, forcing your opponent to forget their plans and put their King in a safe position
- Checkmate - An attack on the King that leaves him no way to get out. Your opponent will not be able to capture the piece that is attacking, move his King or move another piece in to block the attack. Checkmate is the end of the game
- Control – Dominating a particular square or group of squares that are important, for example the center squares
- Defense – A single move or a sequence of moves that defend against an attack
- Development - The process by which you bring your pieces into the game in the opening, in readiness for the middle game
- Discovered Attack – A tactic in which a piece is moved, revealing a hidden attack from a long-range piece, like the Queen, Rook or Bishop

- Discovered Check – Another kind of discovered attack in which a moved piece reveals a check on the King
- Double Attack – When two pieces attack two enemy pieces at the same time
- Double Check – When two pieces attack the King at the same time. These are extremely powerful moves because the opposing player cannot stop the check by capturing or blocking either of the pieces
- Doubled Pawns – A pair of pawns of the same color lined up one behind another. These are weak pawns, as they cannot protect each other
- Draw - The game ends with no side winning or losing
- En Passant - French term for a capture between two pawns. A pawn will move forward two squares on its first move and goes past an enemy pawn on the 5th rank. The enemy pawn may capture the passing pawn on its next move
- Endgame - The last phase of the game when the only pieces left are usually Kings and pawns, with a couple of other pieces.
- Exchange – A swap or a trade of pieces
- File - The vertical row of eight squares

- Forced – A move or sequence of moves that you are forced to play in order to avoid playing a bad game
- Fork - An attack in which a piece threatens two pieces at once
- In Your face Checkmate - The checking piece, with another piece in support, is directly beside the King. This is usually done by a Queen with another piece marking her square
- Kingside – The E – H Files, or the right hand side of the board where the Queen, Bishops, Rooks and Knights start
- Major Pieces – The Rooks and the Queen, also called heavy pieces
- Mate - Shortened version of Checkmate
- Mating Attack - A sequence of moves that are made with the specific coat of checking the opponents King
- Middle Game - The middle part of the game, that slots between the Opening and the Endgame and where both players are looking to take an advantage
- Minor Pieces - The bishops and Knights
- Open File – A vertical row that has no pawns in it
- Opening - The beginning sequence of moves

- Passed pawn – Name given to a pawn that has moved beyond the reach of the other side's pawns and has not got any pawns to the front of it
- Passive - A move that lacks activity and does nothing to fight
- Pawn Center - When the center squares of the board are in occupation by one player's pawns
- Pawn Chain - A pair or more of pawns, both the same color, that are linked diagonally.
- Pin – A tactic in which a piece can't move or they will expose a piece of a higher value that can be captured
- Promotion - When a pawn reaches the 8th rank, it can be promoted into any other piece, usually a Queen
- Queenside - A to D files, or the left hand side of the board where the Queen, Rooks and Bishops start
- Rank – The horizontal row of eight squares
- Resign – To concede defeat and give up the game before being checkmated
- Sacrifice - To exchange or give up a piece for one of a lower value to gain an advantage

- Skewer – A tactic whereby two pieces are attacked simultaneously, with the higher value piece first in the line of fire
- Stalemate - A position where the player whose turn it is to play cannot move legally and is not in check
- Time Control - The time left on the clock to complete the game or to play the given number of moves. Going over the time means losing the game
- Trap – Where you make a move that provokes your opponent into making a bad move. A trap is usually set to entice a player to capture a piece, leaving themselves open to a serious attack
- Trapped Piece - A piece that comes under attack, normally from a piece that is less valuable, and has nowhere safe to go
- Underpromotion - Moving one of your pawns to rank 8 and promoting it to a Rook, Bishop or Knight and not a Queen
- Weakness - A pawn or a square that is very difficult or next to impossible to defend.

Conclusion

I hope that you are excited to practice the different openings and tactics mentioned in this book. As you can see, Chess involves more of planning than intelligence to play, and you should be quick enough to read your opponent's moves and play your move accordingly before the time runs out.

Also, your newfound skills will be sure to attract a larger volume of players to challenge you. Believe it or not, the game of chess entices excitement in people from all different backgrounds. Who wouldn't enjoy pitting their creative thinking against another in a friendly, competitive game? There is a reason that chess has been around for centuries, and it doesn't just have to do with smarts either: it opens the doors to social bonding as well.

Don't start playing by thinking that it is a very difficult game. Agreed that it is a hit amongst scholars, but is simple enough for anybody to take up, including school children!

If you've ever been to a relaxed café, peppered with interesting people, that has a shelf full of games like Apples to Apples, Taboo and Clue; you will be sure to find a chess board among the lot (possibly with some missing pieces). Even though the game itself encourages a sense of mutual dignity and respect amongst its players, in a comfortable setting, it is rife with playful banter not short of smiles or laughs.

If you've been reading this book there is a high possibility that you already have access to a chessboard. I highly recommend taking it and a friend with you on a beautiful day to a public space such as a park, lounge or commons area and begin playing. You might draw attention from passersby who you could invite to jump in on the next game and get acquainted. If you've chosen a prime place, you probably won't be the only people playing either.

It is not possible to become a pro at chess overnight. However, with enough practice, nothing is impossible. I hope this book acts as a catalyst in helping you become a master at this game some day. I hope you enjoyed this book. Thank you again for purchasing this book.

THE END

Dear reader,

I sincerely hope that you feel inspired by CHESS FOR BEGIINERS and enjoyed reading this book.

Before you close this book I´d like to ask you for a favor to leave an honest review on amazon. There are few things more valuable than honest reviews from a wide variety of readers.

Thank you and good luck!

Magnus Templar

CHESS FOR KIDS

How to Become a Junior Chess Master

By reading this document, the reader agrees that
under no circumstances are is the author
responsible for any losses, direct or indirect, which
are incurred because of the use of information
contained within this document, including, but not
limited to, —errors, omissions, or inaccuracies.

Introduction to CHESS FOR KIDS

Chess began about 1400 years ago, in 7th century India, known by the name of Chaturanga. The literal translation of that word means "four" (chatur) "parts" (anga) and this is because the game was made up of four parts of an army – the elephants, the horses, the chariots and the foot soldiers, along with the king and his minister (mantri). In fact, chess began as a battle plan, although a small one and it was devised to come up with ways to beat the enemy.

So, how was this game played? The army on one side was tasked with capturing or knocking out the army on the other side, piece by piece until the King had been captured or placed into 'check' – that means he was trapped with nowhere to move safely. The person who puts the opponent's King into 'check' was the winner. Today, the game is still played that way.

From India, the game was taken to Persia, today known as Iran, by merchants and soldiers in around 600 A.D. and there the name changed to 'Shatranj". At the same time, travelers were also taking the game over to China where the game was modified and called 'Xianqui'. When the Japanese got the game, they called it 'Shogi'.

In the 12th to 13th century, the European crusaders who fought the Holy Wars against the Muslim Saladin in Palestine took the game to Europe and there the name changed to 'chess' - coming from the old French word 'echec' which meant 'check'.

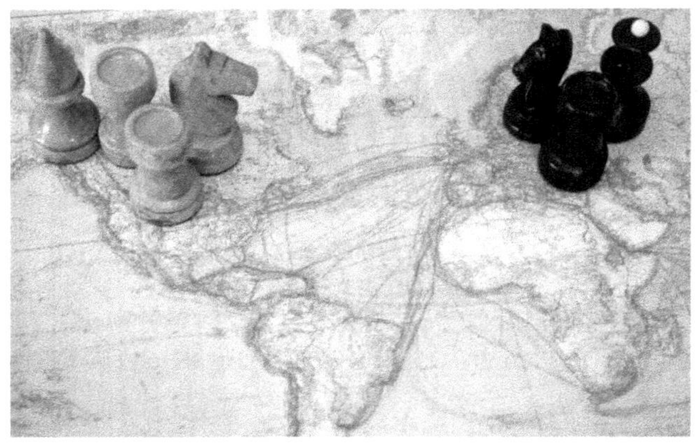

The chess pieces were carved from ivory and they were:

- One King:

- Two Castles or Rooks (the elephants):

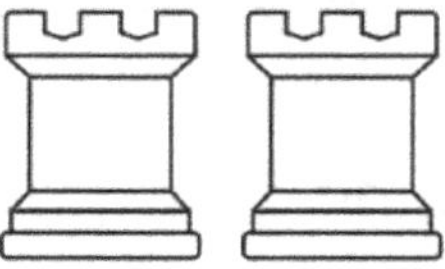

- Two Knights (the horses and the cavalry):

- Eight Pawns (the foot soldiers):

To ensure that they stayed in the Catholic good books (given that it was an incredibly powerful influence at the time) they added two Bishops. The minister was removed and the only female piece of the game, the Queen, was added in.

In no time, chess was one of the most popular games of all times. During the 12th and 13th century Renaissance period, landlords used real people as their chess pieces and those that were captured were beheaded! Thankfully that period did not last long and the game is no longer played like that!

Over time, chess players began to discover that the first movements of their game could determine what the game outcome would be. These moves were known as 'openings' and we're going to look at some of the most popular ones later in the book. Experts began to keep notes on each game they played, on each opponent and began to develop strategies that would preempt the moves that were made.

Chess was never played as a professional game until the 20th century. When they saw how popular the game had become, the media began publishing each game in the papers, move by move and, in 1924, the FIDE (Federation Internationale des Echecs) was formed to come up with rules that supervised how the game was played. Players also started being given ratings for their performances and these were called International Masters. If they became the absolute best, they were given the title of Grandmaster.

It was FIDE that brought the rule into play that every player when they put their opponent's King into a capture position, had to say the word 'echec' or 'check'. At that point, the King was checkmated, and the game ended. The words 'echec mat' or 'checkmate' translates literally to mean 'the King is dead' and this originated from the Persian words 'shah mat'.

Eventually, computers came into the story, making the game much easier to learn and to play. Where an average computer can often beat amateur players, expert players can usually beat the computer.

Today, chess is one of the most popular international games. It was made famous by the Indian Grandmaster Viswanathan Anand. He is joined by other great players, such as Bobby Fisher from U.S.A., Gary Kasparov from Russia and Anatoly Karpov, also from Russia. Once a game, a pastime of the olden days, it is now common to see children aged 6 or 7 playing in international games.

So, without wasting any more time, let's look at the game of chess and provide you with the means to become a junior chess master.

Chapter 1: The Rules of Chess

The best place to start is with the rules of the game and that includes all the moves that each of the pieces can make. The game objectives are very simple – two people play the game of chess, one plays with white pieces and one plays with black pieces. Each player has 16 pieces, made up of:

- One King:

- One Queen:

- Two Castles or Rooks:

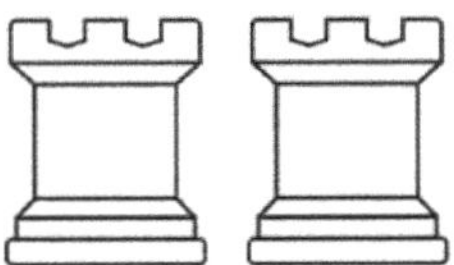

- Two Knights or Horses:

- Two Bishops:

- Eight Pawns:

A chess board consists of 32 black squares and 32 white squares laid out in an alternating color pattern. Each piece will begin the game on a specific square and is moved in a certain way to defend their own pieces from being attacked and to attack the opponent's pieces. The objective of any game of chess is to capture the opposing King. However, it must be noted that the King is not physically captured, only pushed into a position whereby any move he makes puts him in immediate danger. This is known as checkmate, just one of three endings that a game of chess may have:

1. **Checkmate** – the opposing King is put into a position that cannot be got out of without capture
2. **Stalemate** – no player is in a position to win with what pieces they have left
3. **Resignation** – when one player resigns because he or she doesn't have enough pieces let to play with and the opposing player has too much of an advantage.

When the game begins, the pieces are set on the board in a specific way, on the two rows nearest to the player. The row directly in front of the player is laid out as:

Rook Knight Bishop Queen King Bishop Knight Rook

And the Pawns are lined up in front of them as a form of protection:

Pawn Pawn Pawn Pawn Pawn Pawn Pawn Pawn

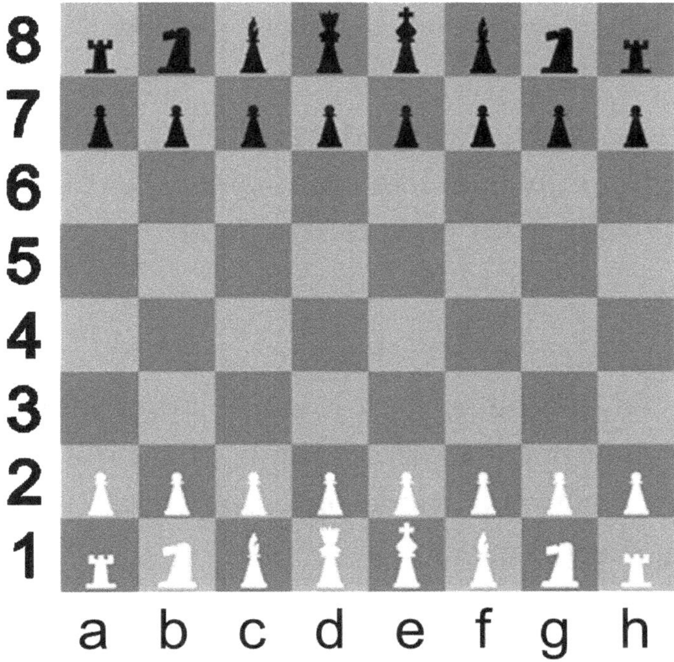

Each of these squares has a coordinate that consists of a letter and a number. We will discuss these in a later chapter. For now, all you need to know is that these are called the rank and file. Let's move onto the pieces and look at how each one moves. This is one of the most important things to learn and master because this is the basis of how your strategy is developed but the strategy is a subject for another chapter.

The Pawns

The Pawn is often treated as a bit of a nobody but, although it may look like a tiny piece it actually has a very big role. Both players start with 8 Pawns, lined in front of the rest of the pieces.

The Pawn has a very limited range of movement compared to other pieces. It can forward only until it gets to the opposite side of the board – if it makes it that far. They may move only one square but there are two exceptions:

* They can move two squares but only on their first move
* To capture an opposing piece, they may move one square diagonally

The Pawn really comes into itself if it can reach the opposite side of the playing board. If you can get a Pawn that far without capture, you may exchange it for another piece except for a King – you can only have one of these, but you can have two Queens if you want and that is the choice that many players make – to swap their Pawn for a Queen.

While we call these pieces the Pawn, they do have other names. Each Pawn is given a name depending on which piece it stands in front of, for example, Rook's Pawn, Bishop's Pawn Kings' Pawn or Queen's Pawn. And they are also named for the side of the board they play on, either King-side Pawn or Queen-side Pawn. For example, at the beginning of any game, the Pawn that is on the left side of the board as you face it would be called the QR-Pawn, or Queen Rook Pawn and, on the right, it would be called the KR-Pawn or King-Rook Pawn.

The Rooks

The Rook is often called the "straight" piece and it looks very much like the tower on a castle. For this reason, it is sometimes called a castle. It begins the game on the two outer corners of each side of the board and each player has two of them.

In terms of movement, the Rook is perhaps the simplest as they can move only in a straight line, sideways or forward. They can move a maximum of seven squares at one time, but they are not able to move over any piece in the way of it. When a Rook is used to capture a piece, it must then be placed onto the square of the piece it takes.

The Knights

The Knight is often called the Horse and its moves are somewhat mysterious. It can only move a set number of squares, but it moves differently. Where the other pieces move in straight lines, the Knight can only move in an 'L' pattern:

- There are just 8 positions on the board that a Knight can move to
- It can move forward, sideways or backward by one or two squares and then must move one or two squares in a perpendicular direction. For example, it may move one square forward and then two squares to the right or the left, or it may move two squares to the right or left and then one square forward or backward
- The Knight may move to any board position so long as that position does not have a piece of the same color on it
- The Knight is the only piece on the board that can jump a piece to get to where it wants to go

The Bishops

Sadly, the Bishops tend to be the most forgotten about piece on the board and, for the beginner, they don't appear to be of much help to you. Each one may only cover half of the board at a time and they are also highly vulnerable to an attack from the front. However, the Bishop is a useful piece, especially for the more competitive player.

Each player begins with two Bishops and you can cover the whole board with them. The Bishop is only allowed to move diagonally and can only move on the color of the square that it starts on. So, the Bishop that starts on a white square can only move on white and the one that starts on black may only move on black squares.

- A Bishop can move diagonally as many squares as it can so long as there are no other pieces in the way
- It may not move past or over any obstruction
- It may capture any piece that may be within its boundaries for movement

The Queen

The Queen is the best and most dangerous piece on the board. She is also incredibly versatile. She is, without a doubt, the most important piece that you have, and you must do everything you can to protect her – lose your Queen, you may lose the game. There are players who will sacrifice every piece to keep their Queen safe.

The Queen moves in a way that is much like a mix of the Rook and the Bishop:

- She can forward, backward or diagonally in straight lines
- She can move as many squares as she wants so long as they are not occupied
- She cannot jump any piece in her way
- She can capture any opposing piece that is in her line of sight

The King

The King is the whole point of the game and every piece on that board is doing one of two things – defending their own King or attacking the opposing King. As soon as your King is in checkmate the game is finished so you need to protect it with all your heart and all your pieces. There are players who try to play and win the game using their King, but this isn't something that beginners should be looking at. No matter where or even if you move your King, you must not lose him.

- The King is the most limited player next to the Pawn and can move just one square in any direction
- He may not move to any square occupied by his own pieces
- He may not move to a square that places him into check
- He may be involved in castling and we will talk about this now

Castling

Castling is one of the more effective chess strategies you will ever need to learn, and it is used as a way of defending your King and keeping him safe. To castle, you move the King two squares to the side, towards your Rook and then move the Rook onto the square that is immediately to the other side of your King. Castling has its own set of rules and it involves just those two pieces, the Rook, and the King:

- For castling to be legal, you must not have moved either the King or the Rook in the game – they must still be in the positions they started from
- There must not be any other playing piece between the King and the Rook
- The King cannot be in check and neither the King nor the Rook may be placed into a position where they can be captured in a move immediately following the castling

En Passant

En passant is a unique rule of chess and many players are simply not aware that it exists. Basically, it only involves the Pawns and it may not even come up in a game. If you were to move your Pawn two squares forward on its first move, there may be a situation where the opposing player's Pawn can capture it diagonally, as if it had only be moved one square forward. The only rule is that it can only be played on a move that immediately follows a two-square start for a Pawn.

Promotion

We mentioned promotion briefly earlier. Provided you can move a Pawn successfully to the other side of the board, you may promote it and choose another piece. Most people go for another Queen, but you can have any piece you like except for a King.

Check

You know what 'checkmate' is, but 'check' is a little different. Check can happen when the King is being attacked and can be captured with the next move but is in a position to get out of the attack.

One rule – you must always inform your opponent when you are going to castle, when they are in check or in checkmate.

And, white is always the starting player.

Never Make Any Move Without Thinking About it

If you are playing a game just for the fun of it, there is always plenty of time to think about what you are doing, to study the play and work out what move to make. Whether you are playing for fun or in a professional game, always, always think before you move because once you move your piece and take your hand off it, that move is final and cannot be changed. If you are unsure, move your piece but keep a finger on the top of it – that way, you can change your mind about your move.

Chapter 2: Rank, File and Chess Notation

Rank and file, we mentioned it earlier, now it's time to look into it a bit closer.

A chess board has 64 squares on it and it is divided up into ranks, which are numbers, and files, which are letters. There are eight ranks and eight files, and each has eight squares. The ranks are the rows on the board and each one is referred to by a number, from one to eight. The numbering begins at the bottom of the board, on the left as you face the board and go up.

The files are the columns on the board and each is referred to by a letter, from A to H, from the left to the right side of the board.

These numbers and letters make it easy for you to identify a specific square on the board by using a method called file-first. For example, the bottom left square of the board is known as a1, short for a-file, first rank. Note that the files use lowercase letters and not uppercase and the reason for this will become clear when we talk about chess notation.

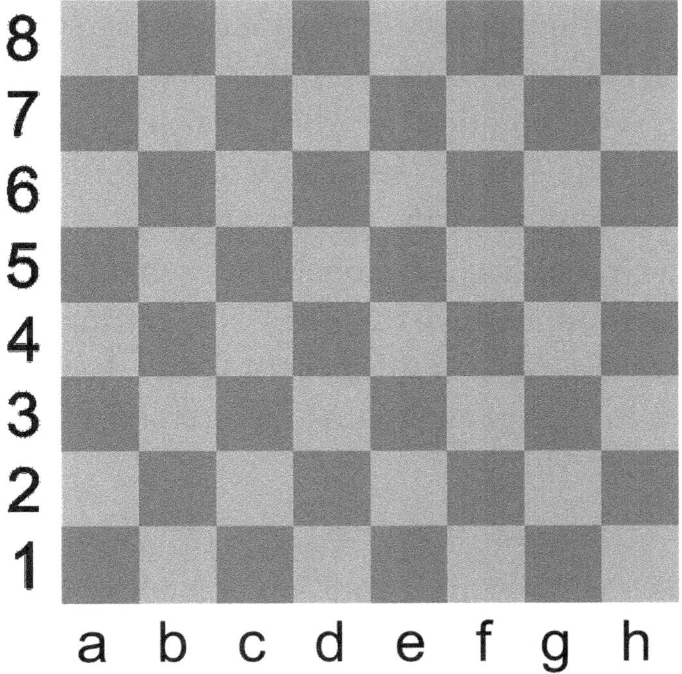

Chess Notation

Chess notation is very important and is something you must learn if you want to become a junior chess master. The notation is what lets us preserve the history of the game, it lets us record all of our games forever and gives us the chance to look back and see how the game has developed into what it is today. The notation is also excellent for getting us over language barriers and in letting us talk to one another in a language that is understood throughout the chess world.

There are lots of different kinds of chess notation; there is the 'forsythe' notation for computer chess games and there are different notations for different languages around the world. However, the one type of notation that is understood the world over is 'algebraic'. This uses a single letter and a single number to give each square its name and uses a letter for each playing piece. These numbers and letters are oriented to the side that the white pieces play from.

Like the numbers and letters or ranks and files as you now know them, each playing piece is given its own notation:

Playing Piece	Notation
King	K
Queen	Q
Bishop	B
Knight	N (K is already in use)
Rook	R
Pawn	Does not have any notation

Note the capitalization; capital letters indicate the name of a playing piece while small letters indicate a square. If a move is notated without a capital letter, only a lowercase, you can assume that the move involves a Pawn.

One of the best ways to see algebraic notation and how it works is to look at what is possibly the most famous and most commonly used openings of all time, the Ruy Lopez opening, the Spanish game. Each of the moves is numbered and there is one move by white and one by black in each of the moves. The Ruy Lopez opening is notated like this:

e4 e5

Nf3 Nc6

Bb5

As you know, white always moves first so the first move is white to e4, black to e5. Remember, because there is no capital letter on the notation, it is a Pawn that has moved. In the second moves, we see that white has moved their Knight to f3 and then black moved their Knight to c6. Lastly, white moves their Bishop into a direct attack on the Knight. The capital B indicates the piece and the small b indicates the square.

With algebraic notation, you can write down any chess move that you can think of and you will be able to understand it because each of the playing pieces is identified as is each square on the board. If you note down every move in the game, it is called the 'score' and you write it on the 'score sheet'.

Special Symbols

Other symbols that you may see in written notations
are:

Symbol	Meaning
X	Captures
o-o	Castle on the kingside
o-o-o	Castle on the queenside
+	Check
#	Checkmate
!	A good move
?	A bad move

You may see more of the last two added, just for the
emphasis.

Chapter 3: Chess Values and Chess Mates

Another important thing you need to learn is the value placed on each chess piece. This isn't too important when you are just beginning but, as you work your way through the ranks, it does become important. The value given to a piece is representative of the power that piece has in the game. Do keep in mind that these values have no technical influence on how a game ends – chess is not won through points! Before we talk further about this, let's look at the values:

Playing Piece	Points
Pawn	1
Knight	3
Bishop	3
Rook	5
Queen	9

The King is never given any points value because it cannot be captured

So, if these values do not affect the outcome of a game, what are they used for? These values are used to provide a kind of estimate about how a game is going. The values may also be useful when you are considering trading pieces. For example, sacrificing one Rook with a value of 5 to take both Bishops with a combined value of 6 would be considered a good trade.

However, only use the values as a rough idea because other things must be taken into account which may change the values. A couple of examples:

- Doubled Pawns have a lower value than undoubled but connected Pawns.
- The combination of two Bishops has more power than the two Knights or a Knight and a Bishop.
- Three smaller pieces that work together, like Bishops and Knights, tend to be more powerful than two Rooks or a Queen.

Elementary Chess Mates

Elementary checkmates happen when a King is alone and is checkmated by the opposition's King and one or more supporting pieces. Some examples include:

1. King/two Rooks vs. King

This is a very simple Elementary Mate. White can do this by pushing the black King, one row at a time, back to the edge. One of the Rooks could be substituted with the Queen and the outcome would be the same.

2. King/Queen vs. King

Unlike the previous Elementary Mate, this time the white King must bring his power into play if victory is to be achieved and he does this by supporting his Queen, the one who checks the King.

3. King/Rook vs. King

A King and Rook together cannot do an Elementary Mate in the same way that the King and Rook do in the previous example. Instead, the white King is used for blocking the 7th-rank squares and the Rook will deliver the Mate on the back rank. You may use a Queen instead of a Rook.

4. **King/Two Bishops vs. King**

The two Bishops work in tandem to push the black King into a corner and the white King is used to stop the enemy from escaping down the side.

5. **King/Bishop/Knight vs. King**

This is without a doubt the most difficult one to learn because the movements are precise. The two principles of this Elementary Mate are:

- The Mate must happen in a square that can be reached by the Bishop
- The Knight controls those squares that cannot be covered by the Bishop

I am not going to tell you the exact movements required because you don't need to know them – these are more for the professionals at the top end of the game and I have only mentioned it so that you are aware of it.

6. **Drawn Game – King/Two Knights vs. King**

It comes as a complete surprise to some players that this game could be drawn but it is perfectly possible. The King can be checkmated but only if there is no reasonable defense put up.

Other Drawn Games

There are a number of games that can be drawn, including:

- King/Bishop vs. King
- King/Knight vs. King
- King vs. King

Chapter 4: Chess Strategies

Strategy is the backbone of your game. It is where everything comes together. The one thing you must not do is to get strategy mixed up with tactics. The two are very different things. Before we go any further, here's why they are so different:

Tactics:

Tactics are the moves, the sequences that you move your pieces in to attack your opponent or to capture their pieces, with the intent of making an immediate gain that counts. When you are thinking about making any move, tactics are the first thing that need to be considered and the most common of these tactics even have names. We will talk more about these in detail in the next chapter but, for now, these are the names you need to remember:

- Discovered attack
- Fork
- Pin
- Removing the Guard
- Skewer

Strategy:

When there is no obvious tactic, the next step is strategy. Tactic is classed as short-term while strategy is more long-term and takes position into account rather than attacking and capturing. Considerations in terms of position are:

- King safety
- Pawn structure
- Piece mobility
- Piece safety

While you should never confuse strategy and tactic, it would be fair to say that, to some small extent, they do rely on one another. Strategy can be used for setting up tactical moves for further in the game and, in the same way, you can use tactics to set up strategy. This all makes things very interesting because this is what the game is all about; tactics, strategy and working your brain, learning strategic thinking and this will have an effect, not just on the game you play now but on your life as a whole.

Three Phases of Chess

A game of chess, if it reaches the end, consists of three phases:

- The opening
- The middlegame
- The endgame

As far as strategy is concerned, each phase is completely different and must be approached as such.

The Opening

The opening accounts for the first moves of a chess game. Often, a beginner will play the first few moves from memory while a grandmaster player may play the first 12 or more moves that way. The opening has three main aims:

- To develop the playing pieces
- To get control of the middle of the board
- To protect your King

Developing your playing pieces requires you to move from their initial positions to the positions that are likely to be the most useful to you. Any piece can be moved but the best ones are the Knights and the Bishops. Once you move the center Pawns forward the Bishops can get out and, by moving a center Pawn two squares forward, you immediately take control of the middle of the board. We'll talk more about the different opening later.

The Middlegame

The middlegame is, quite simply, the part of the game that follows the opening and comes before the endgame. This part of the game is when you start to coordinate all your pieces and begin your attack. The middlegame does not start until your playing pieces have been developed and your Kings have taken part in castling although this part doesn't tend to be rigidly stuck to.

The Endgame

The endgame starts when there are fewer pieces left on the board but, to be honest, there is a fine line between when the middlegame ends and the endgame begins. There are, however, two main themes that will tell you when the endgame begins:

- Pawn promotion
- Your King is in play

Basics of the Opening

Now is when your strategic skills start to come into play but, before you can start concentrating on the openings, you should understand the three principles that go into the opening game:

1. Development

Development is the most important part of this. When you begin to develop each piece, excluding the Pawns, they are being moved from their initial position. You can make good moves, or you can make bad moves. The good ones are those that move the piece to a position that is both useful and doesn't put any piece in danger of capture. Your piece may be developed in response to a threat or by making a threat, however, it isn't the best idea to attack before all your pieces are developed.

The best playing pieces to start development with are the Knights. This is because it is easy to see the positions that they can move to right from the start. Usually, the King's Knight would be moved to f3 or f6 and the Queen's Knight tends to be moved to c3 or d2 or c6 or d7, depending on which color you are playing.

Bishops are useful for helping to control the middle of the board or you can use them to hold one of the opposing Knight's down. The Rooks are best left together at the back – connected, meaning that there are no other pieces between them and they can provide protection for one another.

Do not be tempted to bring out your Queen too early; keep her behind the Pawns and develop her there.

2. Controlling the Middle

This is the next most important thing to remember; it is critical that you get early control of the middle of the board, to set yourself up for a later attack on the opposing King. If you cannot get control, then you will likely fail with any wing attack that you try. The best pieces for controlling the middle of the board are the Pawns and the best moves to make are:

- White – e4 or d4
- Black – e5 or d5

If you use pieces other than Pawns to control the middle, only do it when those pieces can attack from a distance. It's no good developing your Knights and Bishops towards the edges of the board because they cannot play a part in controlling the middle from there.

3. **King Safety**

This is the last principle and is more critical where your game is open, and the middle is not under control. Where possible, castle as early as you can and always castle to King-side where you have a choice.

Basics of the Middlegame

When your pieces, at least most of them, have been developed, the middlegame starts. What this means is that your Knights, your Bishops, and your Queen have been moved from their initial positions, the Kings are likely to have been castled and the Rooks are in the central files. This is where the fun truly starts.

Both players want to be in the number one position, all the while looking for the tactical moves they might be able to make. Middlegame strategy is not quite so easy as it is for the opening and grasping some of the more complex strategies can take years of playing. That said, you do need to know the basics if you want to make it through the middlegame intact so here they are:

1. **Mobility**

In the opening game, you develop the pieces for play but the middlegame is where all your pieces begin to work together tactically. To get yourself in the position to do this, all of your playing pieces have got to be kept mobile, moving all the time as this is the best way to see what's happening and to attack several squares at once.

If one or both of your Knights are playing on the sides of the board then they are not mobile and not in the best positions. Get your knights into the center squares and make sure that they are protected; you will be able to do a lot more with them and you can quickly and easily get over to the side of the board when needed.

If your Bishops have been blocked, they can't move very far and they can't really join in with the game so bring them out, position them on squares where they are on open diagonals and can freely move, covering much more of the board.

If your Rook is left languishing in the corner it isn't doing anything, isn't contributing to the gameplay whatsoever. Get it out into the middle file, the best are those that are open or at least partly open. Open files are those that have no Pawns and a partly open file is one that has an opponents Pawn on it. Positioned correctly, the Rook is a formidable piece and extremely dangerous.

2. **Trades**

In the middlegame, you can start trading pieces but don't rush into this. Think about it, work out of the trade you are looking to make is a good deal for you. For example, if you swap your Queen for a Pawn, it really isn't a good trade, but you could trade your Queen for their Queen; although you both lose your most powerful player, it does mean that neither of you has an advantage. That said, your Queen is not one you should consider trading unless you absolutely have to so try not to put her in that position. There are three times when it makes sense to trade a Queen for a Queen:

- When you have more in value on the board
- When you are under serious pressure
- When the opposing player has a good piece in a good place that is worth trading for

Other than these three times, your Queen should be protected for as long as possible.

3. King Safety

We talked about King safety in the opening game and now we are going to talk about it in the middlegame. King safety is incredibly important throughout the entire game so, if you have gotten to the middlegame without castling and you are in a position to do so, do it now.

Leaving your King in the middle of the row leaves him vulnerable to attack. He has the protection of three Pawns when they are lined up in front of him and, when those are moved, your King is open to attack. While you have most, if not all your playing pieces left on the board, don't move these three Pawns – they will provide the guard for your castled King.

If the opposing King has been left in a vulnerable position, start looking for the tactical opportunities that can lead to an attack. The same applies to when the opposing player moves a Pawn from protecting his castled King.

Basics of the Endgame

The endgame begins when most of the pieces have been removed from the board. In some endgames, you may only have your King and Pawns left on the board while, in others, there will likely be a few other pieces. There are two basic concepts to learn for the endgame:

1. King Activation

Now is the time to bring out the King. For the opening and the middlegames, we did all we could to keep our King safe but now we need him in play. He is, in this stage, the most important piece on your side.

When you no other pieces or only a few, bring your King out gradually – take care because it is still possible for him to be checked. Keep an eye on any Knights on the board and, if your opponent still has a Bishop in play, keep your King off his color; for example, if his Bishop is on white, keep the King on the black.

One more point before we leave this section – activating your King before your opponent does give you a better chance of winning.

Passed Pawns and Promotion

A passed Pawn is one that the opponent cannot stop from reaching the opposite side of the board. This is a big goal in the endgame, to create as many of these passed Pawns as you can. To achieve this, you need to take as many of your opponent's Pawns as you can, either trade them or sacrifice – but only if it is worth it.

Once you have a passed Pawn, you have one more job – to get it to the opposite side of the board in safety and there it can be promoted to another piece. Give your passed Pawns protection by positioning your Rooks behind them and use your Bishops and Knights to block one of the opposition's passed Pawns, to stop them from being promoted. You may also use your King to take a pawn to safety but only if you do not put him in a position where he can be checked.

More Tips for Strategy

- **Don't move one piece twice in the opening game.** Develop a piece and leave it until all other pieces are developed. The only exception to this is if the piece is attacked. This is not considered as a rule violation because your opponent has more than likely moved away from the principle by mounting the attack and that will be an advantage to you.
  However, this doesn't mean that both your Knights should be developed before your Bishop is brought out, but it is better to play your King's Knight before you play your King's Bishop and the same on Queen-side.
- **Don't develop only on one side of the board** – you need to get your pieces developed evenly
- **Don't move a piece beyond the middle of the board in the opening game.** You need all your pieces in place to protect each other when they move onto the enemy side of the board. However, you will find that in some popular openings, like the Ruy Lopez, that this is ignored

but you will understand more about that when we discuss those openings.

- **Try not to make any trades which result in an opponent's piece being developed.** This is ignored so many times by new players, but you must learn it and learn it well because, when you start being ranked on your journey to becoming a junior chess master, you will not get far if you ignore it.
- Try not to trade Bishops for Knights too early. Bishops can move further than a Knight, so you want them in play for as long as you possibly can. It is only in the endgame where the night becomes more powerful because it is not limited to just one-color square like the Bishop is.
- **Avoid making premature attacks** – more games are lost in this way than in any other. Never carry out any attack until you have enough force to carry the attack to a successful conclusion. Premature attacks normally end up coming back on you and not in a good way.
- **Always look for the weaknesses in your opponent's position.** Let's say that both players have developed their pieces properly and that you are now in the middlegame. Eventually, one of you will make a move that could be

considered a bit iffy and that will weaken that player's position. Success in this game depends, to a large extent, on how the opposing player spots that weakness and then pushes his advantage.

Chapter 5: Chess Tactics

We talked about strategy, now let's talk about tactics. Learning and practicing these tactics is absolutely the best way to get ahead in your game and one of the main things to learn is tactical motifs. Tactics are your very first move before you even consider looking at strategy. Tactics are what determines the outcome of any game below Grandmaster level and they are a sequence of moves that tend to include an attack and/or capture of an opponent's piece.

Tactical Motifs

Tactical moves will show up anywhere in a game of chess and they appear in several formats or patterns and these are what we call tactical motifs. If you want to achieve your dream of becoming a junior chess master then you need to learn what these motifs are, how to recognize them on the board and how you can use them to the best advantage. Here we are going to look at 6 common patterns:

- Discovered attack
- Forks
- Knight forks
- Pins
- Removing the guard
- Skewers

This is when we begin to see just how exciting chess is and how much it can boost your levels of concentration and confidence. The more you play and the more you learn, the more you will see your strategic thinking and reasoning skills improving, not just in chess but in all areas of your life. This makes chess a highly rewarding game that provides benefits everywhere in your life.

Back to the tactics. These are sorted into groups, making it easier for you to understand and learn them, one group at a time:

Group One Tactics

Group one tactics are those centered around the fork and there are quite a few of them. A fork is a tactic whereby one piece attacks two of the opponent's pieces at the same time. No doubt you will have seen some of these throughout your time studying the game of chess, or even watching chess tournaments on the TV, you will have seen some of those, most notably the Knight fork; the Knight is one of the best pieces you have for making simultaneous attacks but there are other pieces too:

- **Knight Fork**

This is where one Knight is used to attack two other pieces at the same time. Provided your Knight is positioned correctly, it will easily target two separate pieces, and this is one of the best tactics to employ because you can, if you do this right, attack two valuable pieces, maybe a Rook and a Queen, for example. The reason this is such an effective tactic is all down to the way that the Knight moves, different to all the other pieces on the board. However, there is a warning that you should take note of – never use your Knight to attack your opponent's Knight because you will sacrifice yours.

- **Queen Fork**

There is no denying that the Queen is your most important piece and a Queen fork is where your Queen is positioned to launch an attack on two opposing pieces at the same time. However, be careful with this because, if you don't do this correctly, you could end up sacrificing your Queen and that is something you do not want. You should only use a Queen fork if the result is going to be a checkmate or that you take the opposing Queen – do not use it at any other time. The key to the Queen fork is that you should never use it as an attack on any piece that has protection because it will come back on you and will result in the loss of your Queen so focus on thee targets only:

- Two opposing pieces that have no protection
- The King and one other piece that has no protection

When you target pieces that do not have any protection, your opponent then has to make a decision – which of those pieces do they move to protect? By doing that, they are also making the decision to sacrifice the other piece. However, be watchful when you do this – you might have missed a move that your opponent can make to put your

Queen in danger, thus saving his own pieces and putting you on the back foot.

If you choose to target the King with another piece, the first thing your opponent has to do is remove his King from danger – to do that will require the King being moved or another piece moved into pin and protect the King. We will talk about Pins later.

If you try to use your queen to target any other piece, you will likely lose her, and the game will be turned in favor of your opponent. Do it right and you can start a series of Queen forks that will force the opposing King into a checkmate situation.

- **Bishop Fork**

The Bishop fork uses the Bishop to attack a pair of pieces at the same time. You must always make sure that you have proper protection in place for your Bishop so take care when you are looking for your targets. If you don't, you will lose the Bishop. Usually, you would use a Bishop fork to launch an attack on the King and one other unprotected piece or two pieces that have no protection. Like the Queen fork, when you use the Bishop to attack the opposing King, your opponent either has to move his King or pin another piece to him and that can result in the loss of his other piece. Do not make the mistake of trying to use your Bishop to target the opposing Queen or Bishop because they too can move diagonally, and you will end up sacrificing your Bishop.

- **Rook Fork**

Rook forks work no different to any other fork, you use your Rook to target two other pieces. It is worth bearing in mind that a Rook is higher in value than a Bishop or a Knight so make sure your Rook is well protected otherwise you will lose it. The same rules apply – attack one unprotected piece and the King or two unprotected pieces.

The one thing you should not do is use a Rook fork against the opposing Rook or Queen because that is one battle you cannot win. The Rook is one of your most valuable pieces, next to the King and the Queen, so don't use it unless you have to and unless you are guaranteed to win.

Group Two Tactics

Group two tactics are the Skewers or Pins. Both may happen when your opponent has two pieces on the same line and you are in a position to place a piece that can attack through both. Like the fork, this is another double attack.

Arranging a Pin

Before we discuss the different pins, you must understand what they are. A pin is nothing more than a formation where your opponent is unable to move a piece because he would be exposing another piece with a higher value. There are absolute pins and relative pins.

- **Absolute Pin**

Usually, an absolute pin will come out of these moves:

- When you place the opposing King into check with one of your pieces
- Your opponent should, ideally, move his King out of the way but they could also move one other piece between their King and your piece, thus eliminating the check

However, this will place your opponent between a rock and a hard place. If they subsequently move that piece, they will leave their King unprotected again, so the pinned piece must not be moved. By using this pin, you can threaten the King and render one of their other pieces unusable. And, if that is a piece with a higher value then you get more rewards out of it.

- **Relative Pin**

Relative pins usually result from this sort of move:

- You threaten one of your opponent's pieces
- Your opponent has a choice – either remove the piece under threat or move another piece in to get in the middle

The relative pin is not much different from the absolute pin with one exception. In an absolute pin, the opposing side protects their King with a pinned piece but, in the relative pin, he must protect another valuable piece, like the Queen.

Relative pins are not too much of a threat because they don't involve the King, the most important playing piece you have. Your opponent has the option of sacrificing the piece under threat, thus releasing the pinned piece.

Skewers

Skewers are similar to pins and we often hear them called 'reverse pins'. With a normal pin, you use a lower value piece to protect a higher value piece but in the skewer, the opponent uses a higher value piece pinned before a lower value piece. In a case like this, the opposing player has little option but to remove the higher value piece away from the threat and that leaves you able to take the lower value piece. Normally you would use pieces with a long range of movements like your Queen, Rook or Bishop and there are two skewers that you could use:

- **Absolute Skewer**

So, in a skewer, the higher value piece stands between you and the lower value piece and, with the absolute skewer, the higher value piece is the King. To get out of the check threat, the opposing player must move their King and that puts the lower value piece under threat of capture. Absolute skewers are best done with a Rook, Queen or Bishop.

- **Relative Skewer**

This is a little like the absolute skewer but there is a difference – the King does not get involved. Instead, another piece of a higher value is used, such as the Queen or the Rook, to get in front of the lower value piece. Relative skewers are best done with the pieces with a longer range of movements like the Rook, Bishop or Queen.

Group Three Tactics

The third group of tactics takes in the discovered attack and this will happen when you remove one of your pieces away from another in a way that both of those pieces are in a position to attack two of your opponents' pieces simultaneously. Once again, your opponent is left having to make a choice – which piece to move and which one to sacrifice.

This is a very powerful tactic and can also lead to a discovered check – when you move one of your pieces, you may expose another that immediately checks your opponent's King or, if you are very lucky indeed, puts the King into checkmate. Normally, a discovered attack would be done using the Queen, Knight, Rook or Bishop.

Group 4 Tactics

The fourth and last group of tactics covers any other situation where a double attack can be used. Normally, these situations are when you can put your opponent under pressure or can take one piece that is providing protection for another that you really want. Your opponent has no way of fighting both threats at once, so your threat will result in at least one capture.

- ## Interference

You don't see this tactic in use very often but, should you get the chance and your opponent gets taken in by it, you can take a piece from them. This won't always be the case and, unless you have already previously put him under pressure, he won't often take your bait and the capture won't happen. Here's how interference works:

- You move a piece of a lower value, such as a Pawn, in a way that puts in deliberate threat of attack form your opponent.
- Another piece is backing up your Pawn, so it won't be too much loss if your Pawn is captured

- If your opponent opts for the capture without noticing your threat, you would trade a lower value piece or one of a higher value.

Usually, your opponent won't be positioned to take the bait and it won't be a very effective tactic unless he does.

- **Decoy**

The name kind of spills the beans on this one. All you do is draw out a specific opposing piece, tempting it into the square that you want it to be in, and then you capture it. You would normally do this by using another technique for distraction, like sacrificing a piece that will tempt your target to where you want it.

You must pick your target and then plan your moves around it and the usual series of moves would be something like this:

- Your target will usually be under protection from another opposing piece so that's your first task — to remove that piece. Do this by moving an easy target in for the guard to see; the guard takes it, leaving your desired piece unprotected for at least a couple of moves

- Then, you move in one of your pieces to a place where it will lure the target to move to the square you want, enabling the capture

The decoy tactic has two components – you will lose a piece so don't make it a higher value one and second is luck, you will need some. Luck is the biggest motivating factor because your opponent needs to fall into the trap you set. Failure to do so means your tactic fails. If he does, you have the potential to take on of his important pieces.

- **Battery Attack**

Thee attacks require you to have two pieces in the same file or two in the same line that work pretty much the same. If you chose your Rooks, both are lined up in the same file or, if you opted to use your Bishop, you would have the Queen and the Bishop positioned on the same diagonal. Battery attacks are normally used for these reasons:

- When you are building up a line of power that will help you to capture opposing pieces
- When you want to remove those pieces providing the opposing King with protection and give you the opportunity to check him.

The best combinations for a battery attack are:

- Two Rooks in the same file, lined up
- A Queen and Bishop on the same diagonal
- A Queen and Rook on the same line – either vertically in the same file or horizontally in the same rank

Battery attacks provide you with maximum power as they can provide a constant onslaught, threatening your opponent with no let-up.

- **Clearance Sacrifice**

We use this tactic to get one of our own pieces out of the way of another of your pieces. When you sacrifice the first piece, you open a higher value piece up to move forward and the moves would normally be something along these lines:

- A lower value piece stands in the way of a higher value piece, a Pawn and a Rook for example, and this stops the Rook opening. The Pawn makes the Rook inactive because it can't move anywhere
- The Pawn is moved forward to a position where it is directly under threat from an opposing piece and let it get taken
- The file is now open for the Rook to move

Yes, you sacrifice a piece, but you can make it a lower value piece. Never do this if your sacrifice is a higher value playing piece.

Chapter 6: Popular Chess Openings

Now that we have looked at your tactics and strategy, its time to look at some of the more common and popular chess openings.

The very first moves of any chess game are called the 'opening' and a good one will do four possible things:

1. Provide your king with better protection
2. Give you control over part of the board, the center is best
3. Give your pieces better mobility
4. Provide you with the opportunities to take Pawns and other pieces.

Opening moves have been studied for centuries and most have been given a name that indicates what they are and to simplify any game discussion. In this chapter, we look at some of these openings so that, when you see them being played you can identify them by name. While most chess books will give you in-depth instructions on how to play each of the moves, I will just be giving you an overview of each one and the moves to make so make sure you find other more detailed information to study on each opening before you use it.

All openings have the same principles – to take or control key territories, like the center of the board and to open your pieces in a way that puts them in better and more useful positions. Some of these openings are very direct while others a little lower key. There are three types of opening to look at:

1. White begins by moving Kings Pawn two spaces forward. This has a number of benefits; the center comes under his immediate control and the Queen and Bishop are freed up. This move leaves black with two choices:
   o To mirror the move and move his own King's Pawn two steps forward and this leads to openings such as the King's Gambit, Ruy Lopez, Evans Gambit and Giucco Piano

- o Black could make any other move that would lead to an opening such as French Defense, Sicilian Defense, Pirc/Modern, Center Counter and Caro-Kann
2. White begins by moving Queen's Pawn to d4. This leads to openings like Kings Indian Defense, Queen's Gambit, Bogo-Indian, Nimzo-Indian, Dutch Defense and Queen's Indian Defense.
3. White may make any other move leading to an opening like the English Opening

We discuss these openings below in brief details:

Ruy Lopez

Otherwise known as the Spanish Opening. Starting moves are:

1. e4, e5
2. Nf3, Mc6
3. Bb5

This is one of the oldest openings and was named for a 16th-century chess enthusiast and Spanish clergyman. He studies this opening and many others, recording them all in a notebook which ran to 150 pages. However, although it was given his name, this opening began much earlier. It was found recorded in the Gottingen manuscript which we know can be dated from 1490. However, the Ruy Lopez did not become a popular opening until the middle of the 1800's when a Russian theoretician by the name of Jaenisch rediscovered the potential it had. Today the opening is still used and is one of the favorites of chess great's like Bobby Fischer and Gary Kasparov.

In the Ruy Lopez, white starts by immediately creating what could be a pin of the Knight or the d Pawn and kicking off an early attack while, at the same time, he is getting ready to castle. Generally, white will put pressure on the e Pawn black is playing with and tries to get ready to put a pawn on d4. The best response from black on move 3 is to move to a6 which will launch an attack on the white Bishop. Following that, white can do two things – back up to Ba4 or move Bxc6 to trade.

Giuoco Piano

This is sometimes called the Quiet Game, it involves white using their Bishop to carry out an attack, but it isn't a hard attack and black can usually even things up using his defense. The first moves are:

1. e4, e5
2. Nf3, Nc6
3. Bc4, Bc5

If white were to reply with d3, you would the be playing the Guioco Pianissimo, otherwise called the Quietest Game and this is one of the more passive games of Chess. If, however, white was to reply with b4?! You would be playing the Evans Gambit, a game in which white offers to trade a Pawn for control of the center and has the potential to open how Queen's Bishop.

King's Gambit

This was a very popular opening back in the 1800s and it works like this. White offers up a Pawn in trade for some fast development – that's all there is to it. It is not normally used at master level anymore because it has been noted that it is possible for black to get themselves into a position whereby they don't have to trade anything for the Pawn. The opening moves are:

1. e4, e5
2. f4

The move that would naturally follow this is exf4 and this would be an acceptance of the King's Gambit.

Sicilian Defense

The opening moves in the Sicilian Defense are

1. e4, c5
The Sicilian Defense is used a great deal at master level. Black starts an immediate fight for the middle by, by launching the attack from the c-file rather than mirroring the move that white makes, black is creating an asymmetrical position that can lead to many more positions that are complicated. Black attempts to attack the white e-Pawn, usually using a Knight on f6 and Bishop on b7 – black is looking to move to d5 without any comeback.

The Sicilian Defense has been studied extensively and there are a few variations of it, one of the most popular being the "Dragon" which starts:

1. e4 c5
2. Nf3 d6
3. d4 cxd4
4. Nxd4 Nf6
5. Nc3 g6
What happens here is that black carries out what we call a 'fianchetto' * on the Bishop on the diagonal h8

to a1. It's known as the Dragon because the Pawn structure for black supposedly looks like one.

Another popular variation is called the "Nixdorf" and this one begins like the dragon but changes on move 5 for black:

1. e4 c5
2. Nf3 d6
3. d4 cxd4
4. Nxd4 Nf6
5. Nc3 a6

Daniel King, a Grandmaster, says that white will often respond by moving Be2 giving black the opportunity to attack the middle with e5!

* a fianchetto is when the Bishop is developed up to the second rank of the Knight file that is adjacent, and the Knight Pawn has been moved a square or two forward.

French Defense

Black gives quite a bit of control over the middle of the board to the white, but the trade-off is that black can try to build up a wall of Pawns. The starting moves for the French Defense are:

1. e4 e6
2. d4 d5

Games played with this opening tend to involve a lot of pushing back and forth for position. The middle of the board normally gets closed off and a pair of opposite Pawn chains grow with each player working hard to outflank the opponent. Usually, white will play e5 while black goes for c5 or f6 and the Queens Bishop on black will often end up trapped, pretty useless and tends to be given the name of "French Bishop".

Caro-Kann

Caro-Kann opening is similar to the French defense in that black lets the white side build up control over the middle while black attempts to get a Pawn on d5. It looks a bit like a poor Sicilian and the first moves are:

1. e4 c6
2. d4 d5
3. Nc3 dxe4

Black takes out one the central white pawns and can then get on with developing his pieces, a bit of an advantage compared to the French defense. However, black tends to end up playing a more passive/defensive role in the game so players who start with this opening tend to be looking for the white side to trip up, even slightly.

Center Counter

The starting moves for the Center Counter are:

1. e4 d5

Sometimes you will see this called the Scandinavian opening and, commonly, you will see it continue as

2. exd5, Qxd5

Pirc/Modern

This opening is sometimes called the Pirc and sometimes called the Modern and the opening moves are:

1. e4 d6
or

2. e4 g6
The Modern defense is often labeled as:

1. e4 g6
2. d4 Bg7
This is quite new and, back in the 1930s, it was considered to be a poor opening. However, by the 1960s it was being played quite regularly. Black allows white to take control of the middle but only with the view of undermining that position and ruining it altogether. This is a tricky opening and playing it correctly is actually counter-intuitive because control of the middle is not the goal of the opening, especially as black is doing nothing more than undermining the control.

Queen's Gambit

Queen's Gambit starts with a different opening than e4:

1. d4 d5
2. c4

White stars by putting a pawn on offer in trade for quick development. Black may choose to accept the Queen's Gambit with dxc4 although this is quite a risky move. Black may also choose to play Nc6, which is called the Tchigoran Defense, e6, which is the Orthodox defense or the Tarrasch Defense.

King's Indian Defense

This is one of the more 'hypermodern' openings where back, once again, allows white to control the middle with the intention of ruining the position later. It is risky, but it is a favorite opening for both Gary Kasparov and Bobby Fischer. The opening moves are:

1. d4 Nf6
2. c4 g6
3. Nc3 Bg7

A continuation of those moves could be

4. c5, d5
5. e6, b5

Other Indian Defenses

There are a few other India defenses:

- Nimzo-Indian
- Bogo-Indian
- Queen's Indian Defense

All of these begin with these moves:

1. d4, Nf6
2. c4, e6

Dutch Defense

The Dutch defense begins with these moves:

1. d4, f5
The Dutch defense involves incredibly aggressive counter-play on the side of black by moving straightaway to the white kingside. However, this also provides black with a position of weakness right from the start because moving the f-Pawn creates a hole and stops black from developing their pieces.

English Opening

The English opening is described as a "flank maneuver" and starts completely differently from any other opening:

1. c4
In this opening, white is pushing to control the middle by getting some support from the sides and black will normally counter with c5.

Chapter 7: Common Endgames and Chess Principles

We've looked at openings and later we will look at the principles that surround the opening, middle and endgryames but now, we are going to look at some of the more balanced endgames. These are ones that are frequently seen and are those in which neither black not white has any distinct advantage in terms of material value. I'm not going to teach you how to play correctly in these situations; I am only introducing them to you as a way of giving you something to learn from.

King and Pawn

When it is only Pawns and Kings left on the board, we call it a K&P endgame, or King and Pawn, the major theme of this endgame is passed Pawns. Passed Pawns have got no Pawns from the opposition in front of them, either on their file or on the two files that are adjacent. These are very valuable because they cannot be blocked, and they cannot be captured; they have just one objective and that is to get to the other side and be promoted. On occasion, it will even be worthwhile to sacrifice some of your other Pawns just to create a Passed Pawn. The King is one of the most valuable players in this endgame and should be brought into play as soon as you possibly can during the endgame.

Queen and Pawn

When you only have both Queens and some Pawns left, it is called the Q&P endgame, or Queen and Pawn. One important aspect of this is advanced Passed Pawns. Sometimes, a player who has fewer Pawns can win if he has a higher number of advanced Pawns than his opponent. The player who is at the disadvantage must be continually trying to check the opposite King. Be aware that any Q&P endgame can be very complicated and abnormally long.

Rook and Pawn

This is one of the most common of all the endgames in chess, the R&P endgame, or Rook and Pawn. When the position is balanced this will normally end in a draw and there are a few ideas that you can use as a guide for this ending:

- Attacking Rooks can wreak havoc on the opposing Pawns provided that they can get to the seventh rank
- Defending Rooks should be placed, ideally, behind any opposing Passed Pawns
- Place your own Rooks behind your Passed Pawns to provide them with support in their advance

Bishop and Pawn

B&P endgames or Bishop and Pawn are divided up into two distinct categories:

- The Bishops are the same color
- The Bishops are of opposing colors

When the Bishops fall into the first category, i.e., they are the same color, Pawn position is very important. When your Pawns are on the same square color as your Bishop, you have a bad Bishop because he cannot launch an attack on the oppositions Pawns and his Bishop cannot move very far. When they are on opposite colors you have a good Bishop ad that means you can attack the opposing Pawns and gain control of the gameplay. This will give you a distinct advantage.

Bishops that are on opposite colors will be bad or good and neither Bishop can threaten the other when they are in this situation. This leads to a balanced position and this normally results in a draw.

Knight and Pawn

This endgame, the N&P or Knight, and Pawn, requires some very delicate moves. When one side can create Passed Pawns the defending side has got to block with their Knights, the Knight is a good piece for blocking and this is what tends to end in the game being a draw.

Bishop vs Knight

The BvN endgame, or Bishop vs Knight, is a position that is a little off balance in that each side is controlling a different piece. Bishops are usually seen as the stronger ones, but a bad Bishop may often lose in a duel with a Knight. Also, in blocked positions, the Knight is often a good deal stronger. However, these advantages are very small, and the result is usually a draw.

Top Ten Opening Game Principles

1. Always develop towards the middle to squares that are safe and useful
2. Use your Pawns to occupy the middle and attack using other pieces
3. Castle early, preferably on Kingside to protect your King
4. Develop your pieces to threaten or to defend from a threat
5. Move your Pawns as little as possible and always make those moves to improve piece development
6. Only move each piece once unless you are forced into a position where you must move it again
7. Do not bring your Queen into play too early
8. Work on developing minor pieces before the major ones – Knights before Bishops
9. Connect your Rooks and move them out into open files
10. First move? Move a center Pawn forward

Top Ten Middlegame Strategies

1. Centralize your pieces and coordinate them because this is when you will start to see tactical moves
2. Trade pieces when you are cramped in
3. Trade any pieces that are inactive or bad
4. Never launch a flank attack until you have secured the middle
5. When the opposing King has been exposed, look for combinations, look for tactics
6. When your material value puts you ahead, don't exchange Pawns, exchange pieces instead
7. When your opponent is not developing their pieces well, look for the combinations, and tactics again
8. Attack backward and weak opposition Pawns
9. Get your pieces into the weak opposing squares. Use your Knights to establish outposts
10. Don't move your Pawns unnecessarily in front of your King because you will only weaken your own position

Top Ten Endgame Strategies

1. Get your King activated; it is the most valuable piece you have to play with in the endgame
2. Work on creating a Passed Pawn and get it to promotion
3. When your material value is more than that of your opponent, trade pieces but do not trade Pawns
4. Make sure your Pawns are on the opposite square color to your Bishops
5. Place your Rooks behind opposing Passed Pawns and behind your own friendly Pawns
6. Use your Rooks to cut the opposing King off
7. When the advantage is yours, don't waste your time creating Queen after Queen with Passed and promoted Pawns; instead, use that advantage to press for a checkmate
8. Don't push your Pawns forward prematurely before you have activated your pieces and coordinated them
9. Use both wings to develop your threats and Passed Pawns
10. When the advantage is yours, use it to push for a winning endgame

Chapter 8: The Benefits of Playing Chess

We often hear chess being called a game for those that are intellectual, and it is, indeed, a brilliant game for exercising your brain. And let's face it, the brain is probably the most important organ in your body. Chess is played all over the world by kids and adults alike and while it might not do you any good in terms of toning your body, it will build and tone up your mental health and that will stay with you for life.

Let's look at some of the best health benefits that you can gain from playing chess and these will all help you in your journey to becoming a junior chess master.

1. **Chess stimulates the brain**
Any game that is mentally challenging will stimulate the growth of dendrites in your brain. These are what send signals from the neurons in the brain and the more dendrites, the faster the communication in the brain. Think of the brain as being a computer processor. Each dendrite has little branches inside them and these are what send the signals. They talk to the neurons and this makes that computer processor work faster and better. When you play mentally challenging games, like Chess, those dendrites will grow faster.

2. **Chess provides the brain with exercise**
Challenging games will provide exercise to the left and right sides of your brain. A study that was done in Germany showed that players who were asked to identify chess patterns and geometric shapes used both sides of the brain. Reaction times to simple shapes were the same but the reaction to questions about chess positions resulted in both hemispheres of the brain kicking in.

3. **Chess raises your IQ**
It's true. While there are those who say only smart people can play chess, you could actually look at that

form the other way and say that chess makes you smart. There have been a lot of studies and a high percentage of them show that playing chess on a regular basis can help to raise your IQ. A study in Venezuela on 4000 students showed significant changes in IQ after being given four months of chess instruction.

4. Chess can help prevent Alzheimer's

The older we are, the more our brain's need to be exercised to keep them working properly in much the same way that you would work out to keep yourself and your muscles fit. The New England Journal of Medicine published a study that showed those over the age of 75 who play games like Chess and other brain stimulation games were much less prone to Alzheimer's disease and other dementia forms than those who didn't play.

5. Chess can bring your creative side out

Regular chess paying keeps the right hemisphere of the brain active and this is the side that your creativity comes from. A study that was done over 4 years on year 7 to 9 students involved the students using computers, playing chess and doing some other activities once per week for 32 weeks. The idea was to see which ones were responsible for increasing creativity and the winning group was the one who played chess, with significant changes in creativity, especially in originality.

6. Chess can increase your problem-solving skills

When you play chess, you must be able to think on your feet and you must be able to solve a problem immediately because your opponent will be challenging you every step of the way. A study in 1992 was carried out on 450 5th grade students and the results indicated that those students who already played chess or learned to play it scored much higher on tests than those students who never played at all.

7. Chess teaches you planning skills

When you are a young adult, the prefrontal cortex is the very last part of your brain to develop. This is the bit that is responsible for self-control, for planning and for making best judgment choices. When you play chess, you need two skills – critical thinking and strategic thinking. Chess promotes the development of your prefrontal cortex and it can help younger people to make better choices and decisions throughout their life, stopping them from potentially making risky and irresponsible choices.

8. **Chess improves your reading skills**

How can playing a game possibly help to improve your skills in reading? In 1991, a study was carried out on 53 elementary school students and that study showed that chess does, indeed, improve skills in reading.   Each student was enrolled in a chess program and then underwent an evaluation to compare them to those students who were not playing. The results were definitive – playing chess helps to improve performance in reading significantly. In one district, the reading age was below average but those who were actively playing chess showed an above average reading age.

9. **Chess improves your memory**

Any chess player will be able to tell you that their memory is much better, basically because there are a lot of complex rules and moves that need to be remembered. As well as that, you must have good memory recall skills so that you don't fall into the same traps and make the same mistakes time and time again, as well as remembering a playing style of a particular opponent. Good chess players will have a memory recall and memory performance that is second to none. A study on Pennsylvanian 6th graders ashowed that those students why hadn't played the game before had much better memories after they played along with an increase in verbal skills.

10. **Chess can help you to recover from strokes or other disabilities quicker**

Regularly playing chess can help in the development of your fine motor skills and this never truer than in those who have suffered from a stroke or some other kind of disability that leaves them physically debilitated. Playing chess involves moving pieces, backward, forward, and diagonally and this helps to boost motor skills. Also, because a greater mental effort is needed, an improvement can also be seen in communication and cognition skills. Chess playing can also stimulate concentration and calm, promoting an ability to relax.

Chapter 9: Cool Facts about Kids and Chess

Kids learn to play chess at school

The number of young chess players is on the rise and there are chess camps and school programs all over the place. Much of this increase is down to kids thinking they are just playing a game and the parents and teachers knowing that they are, in fact, learning. Some parents believe that if their child plays chess, it gives them a competitive edge. Excellence in the game can lead to prestige, to recognition and to opportunities for advancement and it didn't take too long for school administrators to jump on board.

Chess has always been important in elite schools, but it is becoming clear that it is also providing the underprivileged schools with a vital advantage too. One thing that has always been maintained in society is that, if you can play chess, you are smart and an increase in self-esteem is taken right back into the classrooms.

Chess teaches a child patience

All children develop at a different pace – some walk earlier than others, some start talking earlier, and others begin to read earlier. Some children take to swimming like a duck to water while others take time to be comfortable. No matter what, being successful at chess means learning to be patient and to sit and think. Kids who are showing elevated levels of kinetic energy can cause disruption at tournaments.

Competitions teach kids how to win and how to lose

Some children will naturally prefer individual competitions while others will prefer to play in tournaments. Competitions can be stressful, so you must be certain that your child can handle that stress. Even kids who are prepared must learn that someone has to lose and to deal with disappointment. Some kids can't accept defeat while others will shrug it off and move on to the next game.

There are those who believe that, if their child cries when they lose it is because they are not ready to enter competitions. In fact, crying is one of the most natural responses; even adult players have been seen crying after a particularly bad defeat. Chess is one way to teach kids how to deal with these things; they are taught that winning is not a given but that what counts is that they give their all, do their best.

Kids can start learning chess from an early age

Most kids are ready to learn how to play chess when they reach the second half of elementary school. There are younger children who show enthusiasm and talent for learning earlier and they will benefit from individual tuition. If they have the right amount of talent, they could think about entering the US Chess Federation National Elementary Championships or they could look at entering the National Junior and High School Championships. There are also other championships open to younger children so keep an eye out for them if your child is showing sufficient talent.

Kids can learn chess online

If you are struggling to find a local chess instructor your child can learn to play by using the internet. There are plenty of reputable sites that are aimed at teaching children chess, many of which provide full training right up to an advanced level, loads of exercises and the chance to play other players online.

Chess can lead to friendships and international travel opportunities

If a chess student continues to improve, they can earn the chance to qualify for a World Team Championship and this is one competition that offers them the chance to compete across the globe, traveling to different countries, meeting new people and making new friends. Some of these friendships last a lifetime while others won't make it past the end of a chess career.

There is a Boy Scout merit badge for chess

You might not believe it but there is one now! Benjamin Franklin was one of the earliest US writers to realize the value in playing the game of chess and, according to him, chess provided improvements to "Foresight, Circumspection, Caution, and Perseverance."

There are scientific benefits to chess

A long time after Benjamin Franklin, academic research began showing an interest in what benefits were offered to chess players. Quite possibly the most famous research of all took place in the 1960's and was carried out by De Groot of the Netherlands. De Groot was responsible for starting the cognitive scientific revolution and his study involved his students being asked to speak their thoughts about their next move from a position that was not familiar. From these interviews, he determined that all chess players had similar thought processes.

Another benefit is called the concept of flow and flow is enjoyable and optimal experiences in which a deep level of concentration on the activity is exhibited. Csikszentmihalyi wrote:

"Flow is what enables people to be satisfied with, and have a sense of exercising control in, their lives. Thus, the flow experience is as typically described as involving a sense of control — or more precisely, as lacking the sense of worry about losing control that is typical in many situations in normal life. In a chess tournament, players whose attention has been riveted for hours, to the logical battle on the board, claim that they feel as if they have been merged into a powerful "field of force" clashing with other forces in some nonmaterial dimension of existence."

Sunil Weeramantry is one of the more successful scholastic chess coaches, an opinionated coach with his own teaching methods. However, we shouldn't all try to be like him, but we should meet certain standards and quite a few States have now adopted these standards.

The Other Benefits of Chess

School children exhibit huge amounts of enthusiasm for chess, children from across the world and the game is representative of a very important cultural institution.

Chess has been the inspiration for literature, artificial intelligence model development and studying cognitive processes. The game can help us to recognize differences between people, to deal with those differences and to deal with losing.

It is a fantastic educational tool, a nice game to play and giving your child the gift of chess may mean you are giving him or her a lifelong gift.

Chapter 10: Glossary of Chess Terms

Active Piece - a piece that can move freely around the board

Algebraic Notation – a system for recording chess moves based on giving each square a number from 1 to 8 and a letter from 1 to h. These are the ranks and files

Battery – two of your long-range pieces, like a Bishop and Queen, both lined up in the same direction on a diagonal, a rank or a file

Blockade – putting a piece in to block a passed Pawn and stop it from getting promotion

Blunder - a poor move that can cost you in material or even the game

Castling - a move that involves your King and Rook. Can only be done if neither has moved, there is nothing between the Rook and King and the King is not placed in check

Centralize – to position your Pawns and pieces for attacking the center

Check - to put the opposing King under direct threat, forcing your opponent to abandon their strategy to save their King

Checkmate – to put your opponent's King into check with no way out

Connected Passed Pawns - at least two Pawns of one color on adjacent files

Control – the domination of an important part of the board

Defense - moves that counter attacks or threats

Development – preparing your pieces for play; this happens in the opening game

Discovered Attack – moving one piece to reveal another that attacks an opposing piece

Discovered Check - moving one piece that reveals another that checks the opposing King

Double Attack – two pieces that attack two opposing pieces at the same time

Double Check – two pieces attacking the opposing King at the same time

Doubled Pawns – a pair of Pawns lined up one behind the other. These are weak as they can't protect each other

Draw – the game ends when no player can win or lose

Dual Purpose Move – one move that achieves at least two things

En Passant – a French term that describes a special capture between Pawns

Endgame – the last part of the game where there are few pieces left in play

Equality – when neither side has a positional or material advantage

Exchange – trading pieces

File - the rows of eight squares going vertically

Force - generalized term for the pawns and pieces

Forced – a series of moves you need to make to avoid playing a bad game

Fork – a piece or a Pawn is attacking at least two opposing pieces at the same time but not on diagonals, ranks or files

Hanging - a Pawn or piece that is not protected and is attacked

Interpose – also known as a block, involves placing a lower value piece in front of one with a higher value to stop it from being attacked or captured by the opposition and usually used to stop your King being captured

Isolated Pawn - a Pawn that has no friendly Pawns on adjacent files

Kingside – the files e to h n the right side of the board where the King, and one each of the Bishops, Knights and Rooks start play

Major Pieces – the Queen, King, Rooks, etc., the bigger value pieces

Mate – shortened version of checkmate

Material – the Pawns and pieces with the exception of the King

Mating Attack – a sequence of moves that you make against the opposing player with one goal in mind – to checkmate their King

Middlegame – the art of the game between the opening and the endgame where both players are looking to gain an advantage.

Minor Pieces – the Bishops and Knights

Occupation – when you put a Pawn or piece onto a square; also used for describing permanent or temporary control of a rank or a file

Open File – the row of 8 squares that run vertically and contain no Pawns. Rooks should be moved to open files where possible

Opening – a sequence that opens the game, such as the Ruy Lopez, English, King's Indian etc. These openings are usually published and have been well studied

Passed Pawn – a Pawn that can no longer be captured by opposing Pawns and has not got any Pawns in front of it

Passive - a move that doesn't do anything or lacks any activity

Pawn Center – when the center of the board is under occupation by one player's Pawns

Pawn Chain – when at least two Pawns of one color are diagonally linked

Pin – a piece that cannot move without opening up a piece of higher value to be captured immediately

Promotion – when a Pawn makes it to the other side of the board, to the 8th rank and can be exchanged for another piece, such as a Queen – you cannot have two Kings though

Protected Passed Pawn – a passed Pawn that has the protection of one of his own Pawns

Queenside – the files a to d on the left of the board where the Queen and one of the Bishops, nights and Rooks start from

Rank -   the rows of eight squares that go horizontally

Resigns - when one player gives up and concede defeat before they are put in the position of being checkmated

Sacrifice – sometimes called by its abbreviation of sac, this is to give up a piece for a lower valued piece to gain the advantage positionally or tactically

Skewer – tactic – two opponent's pieces are under attack simultaneously on the same diagonals, rank or file, with the higher value piece attacked first

Stalemate – a player who is on move does not have his King in check but cannot legally move. Normally classed as a draw.

Tactics – a series of moves that cut down the options your opponent has and can result in good gains.

Time Control – the time left on the clock to finish your move or finish the game. If you go over this time, you will lose your game

Trapped Piece - a piece that is under attack by a lower value piece and has nowhere to go

Weakness – a Pawn or a square that cannot easily be defended

Conclusion

Chess really is a very exciting game and can keep you occupied for hours. Not only is it a fun game, it is also good for the brain, teaching you coping skills for life. As we talked about earlier, there are lots of health benefits to the game and many skills that will help to enhance your whole life.

Learning the game of chess requires a lot of effort and a lot of concentration. You can't play it with half a mind on it because you won't go anywhere; you will constantly lose, and you will never become a chess master. Take the time to learn the rules inside out, learn how each piece moves. Buy a chessboard and practice all the time, play other people or play on the internet. Spend as much time as you can playing and learning, it's the only way that you will get anywhere and the only way that your rating can improve to a level where you can begin to take on more professional players and win.

The End

Dear reader,

Before you close this book, I want to leave you with one last advice.
Get your chessboard out, set it up and start practicing - become the junior chess master that you want to be!
Chess is not limited to adults; kids find it far easier to learn and to retain information, so you stand more of a chance of getting there. Get out there, work hard and become the player you want to be.

Finally, if you enjoyed CHESS FOR SMART KIDS then I´d like to ask you for a favor to leave an honest review on amazon. It´d be greatly appreciated.

Thank you and good luck!
Magnus

www.ingramcontent.com/pod-product-compliance
Lightning Source LLC
LaVergne TN
LVHW010514200726
843506LV00013B/2595